# NEAR

## A 30-DAY DEVOTIONAL JOURNEY
## INTO THE HEART OF PRAYER

# ANGELA ROSKO

# Draw Near: A 30-Day Devotional Journey into the Heart of Prayer

© 2025 Angela Rosko.

**ISBN:** 979-8-9929148-0-1 (softcover)

**ISNB:** 979-8-3507-3426-3 (eBook)

**Library of Congress Control Number:** 2025914247

**Printed in the United States of America**

**First Edition**

**Cover and Interior Design by:** Angela Rosko

**Publisher:** Angela Rosko Enterprises

www.angelarosko.com

All scripture references have been prayerfully selected to deepen your connection with God. While translations may vary, the truth remains the same—He is near, and He is faithful.

This devotional book is intended for personal spiritual growth. It is not a substitute for professional counseling, nor does it claim to offer medical or psychological advice.

# Table of Contents

# Dedication

This book is dedicated to the warriors in worship—the women who lead, nurture, hustle, pray, and rise. This is for every soul hungry for more of God. May these pages fan the flame, deepen your devotion, and remind you that your voice shakes heaven when you pray.

# Preface

## from the heart of Angela Rosko

Dear Sister,

If you picked up this devotional hoping for something real—something that meets you in your busy, beautiful, chaotic life—you're in the right place.

This book wasn't born from a mountaintop experience. It came from the in-between. From the days I felt too tired to pray. The seasons when God felt far. The moments I whispered, "Lord, are You there?" And every single time—He was.

Prayer isn't a performance. It's a relationship. It's messy, holy, honest, and transformational. It's the space where you stop pretending and start communing. And the more I practiced drawing near, the more I realized: He wasn't distant. I just hadn't slowed down enough to notice His nearness.

Draw Near is a journey into that space. For thirty days, we'll explore scriptures that anchor our souls, reflect on what prayer really means, and create moments to listen, surrender, cry, rejoice, and realign. You'll find journal prompts to help you process, affirmations to declare truth, and prayers to guide your heart.

You don't need to be a "spiritual giant." You just need a willing heart.

So come tired, come curious, come hopeful.

Come as you are.

Let's draw near together.

With love and expectation,

Angela

# Introduction

## How to Use This Devotional

Draw Near isn't meant to be just another item on your spiritual checklist. It's an intentional 30-day journey into deeper intimacy with God. Whether you're just starting out in faith or have been walking with Jesus for years, these devotionals are designed to help you pause, reflect, and connect in a meaningful way.

Each day includes:

- **Scripture** – A verse to meditate on

- **Focus** – A one-line truth that highlights the theme of the day

- **Devotional Reflection** – A story or teaching that brings the scripture to life

- **Drawing Nearer** – Guided questions to help you journal and apply the message

- **Affirmation** – A declaration of truth to speak over your day

- **Prayer** – A heartfelt prayer to help you talk with God

You can go through it one day at a time—or spend longer soaking in a devotion that speaks directly to your soul. The pace is yours. The presence is His.

And if you're walking this journey in community, even better! Share your reflections with a friend or small group. You'll be amazed how God meets each woman uniquely yet unites us in His love.

Now, let's begin.

# Day 1

## DRAW NEAR

**Scripture**

James 4:8

*"Draw near to God, and he will draw near to you."*

**Focus:**

Prayer is one way we draw near to God, and this verse promises
His nearness in return.

# Day 1 Devotional Reflection

There's a beautiful promise tucked inside this short verse, a divine exchange that changes everything. God isn't waiting behind some sacred velvet rope, accessible only to a chosen few. He's saying: Come close, and I'll meet you there. That's it. That's the whole invitation. And it's open, daily, for you.

Prayer is one of the simplest, most powerful ways we say yes to that invitation. It's not about having the right words or being in the right place. It's about showing up. Wholehearted. Imperfect. Available. It's your open-hearted presence before a God who leans in when you whisper His name.

But let's be honest: in real life, drawing near can feel more like a luxury than a habit. Between deadlines and daycare, laundry and late meetings, it's easy to feel spiritually foggy or even disconnected. Maybe you're a mom who hasn't had a quiet moment to yourself all week. Maybe you're a professional woman who spends your days making decisions and your nights second-guessing them. Maybe you're a wife navigating relationship tensions with a weary heart. Or maybe you're just tired—and not even sure why.

Here's the good news: God isn't asking you to escape your life to find Him. He's asking you to invite Him into it. Drawing near doesn't mean doing more. It means being more with Him. It means praying in the car between errands. Whispering His name while folding laundry. Crying out to Him in the bathroom between meetings. Letting your real, raw self-connect with a God who promises, "If you move toward Me, I'll move toward you."

We see this promise echoed all over Scripture. Psalm 145:18 says, "The Lord is near to all who call on him, to all who call on him in truth." That means He's not just near to the super-spiritual or the Scripture scholars, He's near to you. He's right in the middle of your truth. Whether your truth today is confident or crumbling, He's not distant. He draws near in both.

Hebrews 10:22 urges us to "draw near to God with a sincere heart and with the full assurance that faith brings." That kind of nearness isn't manufactured but is born out of faith that says, I believe You want me here. When we bring even our hesitant faith, even our distracted minds and heavy hearts, He honors it. He meets it.

And when He draws near, something holy happens. Clarity comes. Peace settles in. Conviction surfaces, but it's wrapped in mercy. When we create space for Him, He doesn't just fill the silence—He fills our soul. Intimacy grows not through perfection, but through proximity. Just like in any relationship, closeness is cultivated through time, honesty, and presence.

So yes, draw near. But not out of duty.  Draw near out of desire. Out of hope. Out of desperation. Out of trust. Out of faith that even in your mess, He is still moved by your nearness.

*You do not have to feel worthy. You do not have to sound poetic.*
*You just have to come.*
*One step.*
*One breath.*
*One whispered prayer.*

**And He will meet you there.**

# Day 1 Drawing Nearer

1. Where in my life do I feel far from God—and why?

   _____

   _____

   _____

2. What does "drawing near" look like in my current season (motherhood, career, marriage, singleness, healing, etc.)?

   _____

   _____

   _____

3. What are the barriers—practical or emotional—that are keeping me from consistent prayer?

   _____

   _____

   _____

4. What is one intentional step I can take today to bring God into the middle of my real, messy, beautiful life?

   _____

   _____

   _____

**Affirmation**

God is already leaning in—I will draw near with confidence, knowing He is near to me.

# Day 1 Prayer

Father,

You have promised that when I draw near to You, You will
draw near to me.
Today I offer a willing heart. Right here, in the middle of the
chaos, the quiet, and the questions.
In the laundry pile. In the long meeting. In the lonely moment.
In the part of me that's tired and the part of me that's still
hopeful.

Lord, teach me how to turn ordinary moments into holy ones.
Open my eyes to see You in the small and sacred corners of my
day.
Let my whispered prayers matter just as much as my shouted
ones.
Let me feel Your nearness not only in the sanctuary, but in the
carpool line, the kitchen, the late-night tears.

Remind me that You're not far.
You're close. You're here.
You're leaning in as I reach out.

And as I take one small, trembling step toward You today—just
one—I trust that You are already running toward me with arms
wide open.

I don't have to chase You down. I just have to turn my face toward You.

Because You're the God who meets me in the middle. Every single time.

Thank You for being near—closer than my breath, closer than my fears.

May Your presence become my peace, and Your love my resting place.

In Jesus' name,
Amen

# Day 2

## BE STILL

**Scripture**

Psalm 46:10

*"Be still and know that I am God."*

**Focus**

Prayer teaches us to slow down and rest in His sovereignty.

# Day 2 Devotional Reflection

"Be still." Two little words that are wildly countercultural in today's high-speed world. Stillness feels foreign when our days are crammed with tasks, texts, and to-dos. But the deeper invitation of this verse is more than silence. It's surrender.

Stillness is not the absence of motion. It's the presence of trust. It's the soul-level pause that says, God, I don't have to carry it all. When we pray, we don't just talk. We slow. We listen. We breathe. We surrender the urge to control, fix, or strive. And in that quiet surrender, we begin to know Him, not just in theory, but in experience.

This is especially hard for the achievers among us. The women who run households, manage teams, juggle finances, and take care of everyone else. Maybe you're a high-capacity woman who thrives on results. You're the one people turn to. The one who gets things done. But even the strongest shoulders weren't built to bear the world.

Stillness invites you to stop producing long enough to receive. It's God's way of reminding us: You are not the source. I am. Prayer becomes the holy exhale, the space where our minds rest and our hearts remember who's truly in control.

We see this holy rest modeled throughout Scripture. In Exodus 14:14, as the Israelites panicked at the Red Sea, God told Moses, "The Lord will fight for you; you need only to be still." That wasn't passive advice. It was an active surrender, a bold trust in divine intervention. Stillness didn't mean doing nothing. It meant stepping aside so God could do everything.

In Isaiah 30:15, God says, "In repentance and rest is your salvation, in quietness and trust is your strength." That quietness is not weakness. It is holy resilience. It is the kind of trust that grows roots in storms and peace in chaos. It is knowing that God is not just with us, He is for us—and that is enough.

And don't miss this: stillness doesn't always look like a peaceful mountaintop moment. It can look like putting your phone down when you're overwhelmed. It can look like sitting in the car an extra five minutes, choosing breath over burnout. It can look like saying, "God, I don't know what to do next," and letting that sentence hang in the air, unfilled by your own effort.

In that sacred stillness, we don't lose ground. We gain perspective. We don't fall behind. We fall into grace.

*You do not have to feel worthy. You do not have to sound poetic.*
*You just have to come.*
*One step.*
*One breath.*
*One whispered prayer.*

**And He will meet you there.**

# Day 2 Drawing Nearer

1. When was the last time I truly felt still in God's presence—and what keeps me from experiencing that more often?

   _____

   _____

   _____

2. What fears or responsibilities make it hard for me to release control and rest in God's sovereignty?

   _____

   _____

   _____

3. How does my busyness affect my ability to hear from God or feel close to Him?

   _____

   _____

   _____

4. What specific boundaries or habits can I create to build stillness into my daily routine?

   _____

   _____

   _____

**Affirmation**

I release the need to rush—God meets me in stillness with peace and presence.

# Day 2 Prayer

God,

You are not rushed. You are not hurried.
You are not pacing the heavens in worry or scrambling to fix what I cannot control.
You are steady. Sovereign. Still.
And today, you're not asking me to do more. You're asking me to stop.

To stop striving.
To stop spinning.
To stop assuming the weight of the world was ever mine to carry.

Teach me what stillness really means—not just silence, but surrender.
Not just slowing down my body, but quieting my soul.
Help me resist the lie that hustle equals worth or that busyness is holiness.
Remind me that You delight in presence, not performance.

I release the illusion of control—the need to fix, to manage, to plan every outcome.
I place it all into Your capable hands: my schedule, my worries, my people, my heart.

And as I breathe deep, I declare that You are already holding what I can't.

Lord, meet me in the stillness.
Speak to me in the pause.
Show me how to trust You—not just in the big moments, but in the in-between.

Let Your peace wash over every anxious thought, every clenching fear, every racing heartbeat.
Still me—until I can hear the quiet whisper of Your voice again.
Still me—until I remember that You are God, and I am held.

And when the world picks up its pace again tomorrow,
Let me carry Your stillness within me.

In Jesus' name,
Amen

# Day 3

## TUNE IN

**Scripture**

John 10:27

*"My sheep listen to my voice; I know them, and they follow me."*

**Focus**

Prayer is where we tune our hearts to recognize His voice.

# Day 3 Devotional Reflection

When Jesus says, "*My sheep listen to my voice; I know them, and they follow me*," He's not just describing a habit. He's describing a relationship. This verse reveals the intimacy God desires with us: to be known by Him and to know His voice so well that we follow Him instinctively.

Listening to God begins with recognizing that He already knows us deeply, fully, and lovingly. He knows when our hearts are weary. He knows the inner struggles we don't speak out loud. He even knows the desires we haven't dared to pray for. Prayer becomes the sacred space where His knowing meets our longing, and His voice meets our need.

As wives, we often pray about our marriages seeking guidance, peace, connection, or healing. But what if the very answers we seek are waiting on the other side of listening? God's voice doesn't just comfort. It convicts, corrects, and directs us into obedience. And obedience is never about control. It's about alignment. When we hear and follow His voice, we walk in the paths that lead to life, peace, and wisdom.

Imagine the power of a marriage that is shaped by that kind of obedience. When a wife chooses to respond to God's whisper—to forgive first, to speak life instead of criticism, to love when it's hard—she's building her marriage on a divine foundation. Not because she's perfect, but because she's listening.

His voice anchors us when emotions rise, when confusion creeps in, or when selfishness tempts us to withdraw. It doesn't always shout. Sometimes it sounds like a quiet conviction or a sudden peace. But when we train our hearts through prayer to recognize His voice, we begin to follow not just out of duty, but out of love.

Jesus also said, *"Whoever belongs to God hears what God says"* (John 8:47). Hearing Him is one of the evidences that we are His. But hearing is not passive, it is cultivated. Just like any close relationship, it requires familiarity, trust, and repeated time together. That kind of spiritual attentiveness doesn't come from rushing through a checklist. It grows from learning how to sit, to listen, and to discern His whisper amidst the noise.

In Isaiah 30:21, God promises, *"Whether you turn to the right or to the left, your ears will hear a voice behind you, saying, 'This is the way; walk in it.'"* That is the gift of guidance we gain through surrendered listening. We begin to move in a direction that flows not from anxiety or fear, but from knowing the Shepherd's voice.

And here's the truth: your heart already knows the sound of His voice. Sometimes you just need the stillness to hear it again. He hasn't stopped speaking. He's simply waiting for you to lean in.

*You do not have to feel worthy. You do not have to sound poetic.*
*You just have to come.*
*One step.*
*One breath.*
*One whispered prayer.*

**And He will meet you there.**

# Day 3 Drawing Nearer

1. How does knowing that God sees and knows me completely impact the way I approach prayer?

_____

_____

_____

2. What is God currently speaking to me about that requires obedience or surrender?

_____

_____

_____

3. How has obedience to God's voice affected my marriage (or my role in relationships)?

_____

_____

_____

4. What distractions do I need to quiet in order to tune into His voice more clearly?

_____

_____

_____

**Affirmation**

God knows me, and I am learning to recognize and follow His voice.

# Day 3 Prayer

Lord,

You are always speaking.
Not just through grand gestures or dramatic signs,
but in the quiet, the ordinary, the everyday moments where I
least expect You.
And yet—how often do I miss it?

My mind is so full.
My world so loud.
My soul so easily distracted by responsibilities, screens, noise,
and fear.
But today, I want to hear You again.
To truly *tune in*—not just listen with my ears, but with my
spirit.

You said Your sheep know Your voice.
Help me remember what Yours sounds like.
Not the voice of shame, but the voice of grace.
Not accusation, but affirmation.
Not confusion, but clarity.
You don't shout to compete. You whisper to draw me near.

So, I quiet myself before You.
I lay down the mental lists, the emotional clutter, the swirling

questions.

I open the door to Your presence and say: Speak, Lord.
Your daughter is listening.

Let Your voice cut through the noise today.
Let it call me back to what matters.
Let it correct me in love, encourage me in truth, and align me
with heaven's rhythm.

And when You speak, give me the courage to follow—without
delay, without excuse, without fear.
Because I trust that You are leading me into peace, not
pressure.
Into purpose, not performance.
Into deeper intimacy with the One who knows me best.

In Jesus' name,
Amen

# Day 4

## ALIGNING WITH HIS HEART

**Scripture**

Micah 6:8

*"What does the Lord require of you? To act justly and to love mercy and to walk humbly with your God."*

**Focus**

Prayer aligns our hearts with His divine values.

# Day 4 Devotional Reflection

We live in a world that constantly pushes us to choose a side, take a stance, lead with confidence, and speak with authority. But in Micah 6:8, God lays out a radically different leadership blueprint: justice, mercy, and humility. Not just in public, but in private. Not just in outcomes, but in the posture of our hearts.

And this is where prayer becomes our greatest leadership tool. Not to ask for power or position, but to realign with the heart of God.

Whether you're managing a team, mentoring younger women, serving your church or community, or simply navigating the leadership that comes with being a mother, teacher, or entrepreneur, your influence carries weight. But if we're not careful, leadership can slowly shift our focus inward. We start making decisions based on performance, pressure, or people-pleasing rather than God's values.

Prayer brings us back. It recalibrates the compass. In the quiet, we begin to see situations differently. We learn to lead not by force, but by faith. To speak with mercy. To act with justice. To walk humbly, knowing that who we are in Christ matters more than what we do for others.

Jesus led this way. He loved people deeply and confronted injustice boldly, yet He did it all from a place of oneness with the Father. When we pray, we take on His posture. We surrender the need to always be right and instead seek to be righteous. We begin to lead from overflow, not exhaustion. From divine alignment, not worldly ambition.

Philippians 2:3-5 reminds us, "*Do nothing out of selfish ambition or vain conceit. Rather, in humility value others above yourselves... In your relationships with one another, have the same mindset as Christ Jesus.*" That mindset begins in prayer. In prayer, we lay down ego and pick up empathy. We stop performing and start abiding.

James 3:17 describes the wisdom that comes from God as "*first of all pure, then peace-loving, considerate, submissive, full of mercy and good fruit, impartial and sincere.*" This is the fruit of a prayerful leader. A woman who leads from a well-watered soul produces fruit that lasts.

And don't miss this: walking humbly with God doesn't mean shrinking back. It means standing firm with your spirit anchored in grace. It means being confident in who God is and who He says you are. Humility is not weakness. It is strength under submission. And it is cultivated in the quiet presence of God.

*You do not have to feel worthy. You do not have to sound poetic.*
*You just have to come.*
*One step.*
*One breath.*
*One whispered prayer.*

**And He will meet you there.**

# Day 4 Drawing Nearer

1. Which of these values—justice, mercy, humility—am I being called to embody more fully right now?

   _____

   _____

   _____

2. Where in my leadership or influence do I need realignment with God's heart and priorities?

   _____

   _____

   _____

3. How can prayer help me lead with both conviction and compassion?

   _____

   _____

   _____

4. In what areas have I been more focused on results than relationship with God?

   _____

   _____

   _____

**Affirmation**

I walk in step with God, reflecting His heart through justice, mercy, and humility.

# Day 4 Prayer

God,

There's a way that looks wise in the world—but You've called
me to something higher.
You're not asking me to lead from ego or ambition,
but from a heart that reflects *Your* heart.

You've shown me what You require:
To act justly.
To love mercy.
To walk humbly with You.

And honestly, God, that's not always my default.
Sometimes I lead from pressure.
Sometimes I seek affirmation from others more than alignment
with You.
Sometimes I chase productivity instead of presence.
But You're calling me back—not to hustle harder, but to
embrace a holy rhythm.

So today, Lord, I lay down my title, my to-do list, my desire to
be impressive.
Strip away the parts of me that are performing for applause.
Realign my motives with heaven's mission.

Let prayer be the space where I'm reshaped—
Not to be liked, but to be like You.
Make me a woman who leads from overflow, not exhaustion.
Who speaks truth with grace.
Who serves with joy, not resentment.
Who corrects with love, not superiority.

Let me be a living echo of Your justice, Your mercy, and Your humility.
Not just in ministry, but in motherhood.
Not just in public, but in private.
Not just in principle, but in practice.

Align my heart with Yours, God.
And let my life reflect You fully.

In Jesus' name,
Amen

# Day 5

## RECEIVING THE OUTPOURING

**Scripture**

Romans 5:5

*"God's love has been poured out into our hearts through the Holy Spirit, who has been given to us."*

**Focus**

Prayer opens us to experience and receive His outpouring.

# Day 5 Devotional Reflection

Sometimes the hardest thing to do isn't giving love. It's receiving it.

Especially when your heart's been bruised. When the people who should've poured into you only drained you. When you've been self-reliant for so long that the idea of simply receiving feels foreign. But Romans 5:5 offers a truth that's not just healing. It's holy: God has already poured His love into you. Through the Holy Spirit. It's not a trickle. It's an outpouring.

But here's the catch. Even divine love can go unnoticed if we never pause to receive it. And that's what prayer invites us into—a posture of holy reception. Not striving. Not earning. Receiving.

Jesus modeled this so perfectly. Even as the Son of God, He constantly withdrew to be with the Father, to receive love, direction, and strength. In the garden, when sorrow threatened to crush Him, He didn't power through alone. He poured His heart out in prayer—and in return, Heaven strengthened Him. If He needed to receive, how much more do we?

For the woman who's been carrying silent wounds, guarding her heart out of survival, or numbing herself just to function—God sees you. He's not waiting for you to break down the door. He's pouring love through it. The Holy Spirit is already within you, ready to flood the parts of your heart that feel dry, abandoned, or unreachable.

Prayer is where that flood flows freely. It's where you unclench your fists, soften your defenses, and say, "God... I'm ready to receive." Not because you've done everything right, but because He's already done everything necessary.

Zephaniah 3:17 says, "*The Lord your God is with you... He will take great delight in you... He will rejoice over you with singing.*" That is the sound of a God who is not tolerating you. He is delighting in you. You are not just accepted. You are adored.

And in Ephesians 3:17-19, Paul prays that we would be "*rooted and established in love... to grasp how wide and long and high and deep is the love of Christ.*" That kind of love is not something we achieve. It is something we learn to receive. It anchors us. It transforms us. It becomes the wellspring of everything we pour out.

You don't have to earn this love. You don't have to hustle for it. You don't even have to understand it fully. You just have to open your hands and heart, and let it in.

*You do not have to feel worthy. You do not have to sound poetic. You just have to come.*

*One step.*

*One breath.*

*One whispered prayer.*

**And He will meet you there.**

# Day 5 Drawing Nearer

1. What keeps me from fully receiving God's love? Are there wounds or walls I still hold onto?

_____

_____

_____

2. When was the last time I felt God's love as more than just a concept, but a real experience?

_____

_____

_____

3. How can I create more moments of stillness in prayer to *receive* rather than just *request*?

_____

_____

_____

4. What would change in my life—and in how I love others—if I truly believed I was fully loved by God?

_____

_____

_____

**Affirmation**

God's love is not scarce—it flows freely in me and through me.

# Day 5 Prayer

Lord,

Sometimes I forget that I'm already loved.
Already filled. Already chosen.
I keep trying to prove something You've already declared.

But today... I stop.
I stop striving to earn what You've freely poured out.
I stop pretending I don't need it.
And I stop minimizing my emptiness as if it's a badge of
strength.

Because You see it all.
The fatigue behind my smile.
The disappointment I've pushed down.
The heart that's been stretched too thin.

And yet You say: *I've already poured My love into you.*
Not with hesitation. Not sparingly. But with wild, generous
abandon.
Through the Spirit.
Through grace.
Through every sunrise that says, "I haven't forgotten you."

So, I make space today.

Not to perform, but to *receive.*

To open my hands, my heart, my mind, and let You pour in again.

Pour into the cracked places. The weary places. The quiet aches I haven't even named.

Teach me to receive without guilt.

To believe without doubt.

To live like a daughter—full, loved, and held.

Let Your outpouring flow through me, spilling into how I parent, lead, rest, and worship.

Fill me again, God.

Fill me to overflow.

In Jesus' name,

Amen

# Day 6

## RESHAPING DESIRES

**Scripture**

Psalm 37:4

*"Delight yourself in the Lord, and he will give you the desires of your heart."*

**Focus**

Prayer deepens our delight in God and reshapes our desires.

# Day 6 Devotional Reflection

Let's talk about desire. Because let's be real—most of us have it. Whether it's a dream to write the book, launch the business, get the promotion, find love, grow the family, or heal from something heavy, we all long for things. Deeply. And sometimes we worry that if we get too spiritual, we'll have to give those desires up.

But Psalm 37:4 says something different. It says: delight in Him, and then—then—He gives you the desires of your heart.

Here's the key: prayer doesn't erase your desires. It purifies them. It shifts them from being all about us to being all about Him. It deepens your delight in God so much that what you long for starts to change. Your dreams get wiser. Your timing gets softer. Your motives get holier. You still dream—but you dream with God, not around Him.

Jesus modeled this beautifully in Gethsemane. In His humanity, He desired relief, *"Let this cup pass from me."* But in His prayer, His heart aligned with the Father's: *"Yet not my will, but Yours be done"* (Matthew 26:39). His desire didn't vanish. It got reshaped by surrender. And because of that prayer, we were all given access to eternal life.

That's the power of prayed-through desire. It stops being fragile. It becomes fortified.

James 4:3 gives us insight too: *"When you ask, you do not receive, because you ask with wrong motives."* That verse isn't to shame us. It's an invitation to go deeper. To let prayer become the place where our wants get washed in wisdom. Where our dreams aren't dismissed but discipled.

And do not miss this: God is not threatened by your desire. He planted it in you. He delights in you delighting in Him. In fact, He wants to partner with you in those longings, not police you for having them. As you pray, those desires become part of the refining fire—burning away the selfish and igniting the sacred.

Proverbs 16:3 says, *"Commit to the Lord whatever you do, and He will establish your plans."* That word "commit" means to roll it onto Him. To place the full weight of your hopes into His care. That kind of commitment flows naturally when your delight is in the Giver, not just the gift.

So, if you are a woman with dreams (and you are), don't be afraid to bring them into prayer. Lay them out. Offer them up. And then delight in the One who sees the full picture. He may shift your desires—or He may surprise you and fulfill them in a way that's even better than what you imagined.

*You do not have to feel worthy. You do not have to sound poetic.*
*You just have to come.*
*One step.*
*One breath.*
*One whispered prayer.*

**And He will meet you there.**

# Day 6 Drawing Nearer

1. What are the deepest desires of my heart in this season—and how have I been holding them before God?

   _____

   _____

   _____

2. Is there any part of my dream or desire that God may want to reshape or refine?

   _____

   _____

   _____

3. What would it look like to truly delight in God—more than the outcome I'm hoping for?

   _____

   _____

   _____

4. Can I trust God enough to surrender my desires, knowing He only gives what's good and right for me?

   _____

   _____

   _____

**Affirmation**

As I delight in God, He shapes my heart and fulfills it in ways beyond my imagination.

# Day 6 Prayer

Father,

There are things I want so badly.
Dreams I've nurtured in silence.
Prayers I've whispered through tears.
Hopes I've carried in secret corners of my heart—some for
years.

And You see every one of them.

But I don't want to chase desires that lead me away from You.
I don't want to pursue dreams that feed my pride but starve my
soul.
So I come to You with open hands and a willing heart.

You said if I delight in You, You'll give me the desires of my
heart.
So Lord, teach me to *delight first.*
To find joy in You—not just what You can do, but who You
are.
To enjoy the sweetness of Your presence before the satisfaction
of answered prayer.

And as I delight, reshape what needs reshaping.
Burn away any selfish ambition, impure motive, or fear-driven

pursuit.

Refine my hopes until they reflect Your wisdom.

Reframe my goals until they align with Your purpose.

I trust You with my dreams.

The ones You planted, the ones You're pruning, and the ones You're preparing.

I surrender the timing, the path, the outcome.

And if the answer is not yet—or not at all—

Let me still be found delighting in You.

In Jesus' name,

Amen

# Day 7

## ANCHORED IN PEACE

**Scripture**

Isaiah 26:3

*"You will keep in perfect peace those whose minds are steadfast, because they trust in you."*

**Focus**

Prayer cultivates trust and ushers in God's peace.

# Day 7 Devotional Reflection

There's a kind of peace the world just can't replicate. It's not spa-day calm or temporary relief from stress. It's perfect peace. The kind of peace that holds steady in the face of unknowns. The kind that doesn't depend on answers, but on alignment.

Isaiah 26:3 promises that peace flows from trust, and trust is birthed and built through prayer.

Maybe you're in a season of transition. A job shift. A move. A new diagnosis. Maybe you're waiting for clarity or walking through uncertainty, unsure of what the next month, or even the next hour, will hold. And every time you try to "figure it out" the peace slips through your fingers like sand.

But prayer changes that. Prayer takes your swirling thoughts and sets them on something steady. It doesn't always give answers, but it always gives access—to a God who is unshakable, faithful, and already ahead of you.

Even Jesus, in the boat during the storm, modeled what peace looks like. While the disciples panicked, Jesus slept. He trusted the Father completely. And when they woke Him in fear, He spoke peace over the waves: *"Peace, be still"* (Mark 4:39). He wasn't just calming the storm outside. He was modeling what it looks like when your soul is anchored on the inside.

Philippians 4:6-7 reminds us, *"Do not be anxious about anything, but in every situation, by prayer and petition, with thanksgiving, present your requests to God."* And here's the promise: *"the peace of God, which transcends all understanding, will guard your hearts and your minds in Christ Jesus."* That word "guard" is military language—it means to stand watch. God's peace is not passive. It's protective. It surrounds you like a shield when life feels unsafe.

Colossians 3:15 says, *"Let the peace of Christ rule in your hearts."* That means His peace can take authority over the chaos, over the spiraling thoughts, over the fear that whispers worst-case scenarios in the dark. And when peace rules, panic loses its power.

You may not be able to stop the storm around you. But through prayer, you can invite peace within you. Peace that stands guard over your mind. Peace that quiets the noise. Peace that flows— not from knowing everything—but from knowing the One who does.

*You do not have to feel worthy. You do not have to sound poetic.*
*You just have to come.*
*One step.*

*One breath.*
*One whispered prayer.*

**And He will meet you there.**

# Day 7 Drawing Nearer

1. Where am I struggling to trust God fully in this season? What specific fears are surfacing?

   _____

   _____

   _____

2. What has prayer taught me about peace—and how can I lean into that more intentionally?

   _____

   _____

   _____

3. What practical steps can I take to set my mind on God when anxiety creeps in?

   _____

   _____

   _____

4. When I look back, where have I seen God's peace carry me through uncertainty?

   _____

   _____

   _____

**Affirmation**

I trust God fully, and His perfect peace guards my heart and mind.

# Day 7 Prayer

Prince of Peace,

There's a part of me that wants to hold it all together—
to plan every detail, predict every outcome, protect myself from
disappointment.
But no matter how hard I try, I can't outrun the waves.
They still crash in.

So today I let go of the illusion of control,
and I anchor myself in You.

You are not surprised by my stress.
You're not intimidated by my questions.
You don't require me to be unbothered—
You just invite me to *trust*.

You said You would keep me in perfect peace if my mind is
stayed on You.
So I bring You my runaway thoughts.
My spiraling fears.
My tight-chested tension.

I place them all before You,
and I ask:
Still the storm in me.

Speak, "Peace, be still," not just over the winds outside—but over the chaos within.

Let prayer be where my perspective resets.
Let it be where Your promises grow louder than my problems.
Let it be where I stop rehearsing worst-case scenarios and start remembering Your faithfulness.

You've carried me before.
You'll carry me again.
And this time, I'll rest while You steer.

In Jesus' name,
Amen

# Day 8

## FAITHFULLY AND WONDERFULLY MADE

**Scripture**

Hebrews 11:6

*"But without faith it is impossible to please Him, for he who comes to God must believe that He is, and that He is a rewarder of those who diligently seek Him."*

**Focus**

Prayer helps us believe what God says about us—even when we struggle to believe it ourselves.

# Day 8 Devotional Reflection

There are days when the mirror reflects more than just our physical appearance. It echoes our deepest insecurities. We question our worth, our purpose, and sometimes even our place in God's grand design. In these moments, it's vital to anchor ourselves in the unwavering truth of Scripture.

Psalm 139:14 declares, *"I praise You because I am fearfully and wonderfully made; Your works are wonderful, I know that full well."* This isn't a mere poetic expression. It's a divine affirmation of our intrinsic value. God, the Master Craftsman, intricately designed each of us with purpose and intention. Every detail, every feature, every nuance was crafted by His loving hands.

Yet, believing this truth requires faith. Hebrews 11:6 reminds us that faith is essential to please God. It is not about having unwavering confidence in ourselves but about placing our trust in Him. Faith means believing that God's words about us are true, even when our feelings suggest otherwise. It is about seeking Him diligently and trusting that He rewards our pursuit with revelations of our true identity in Him.

Jeremiah 29:13 echoes this promise: "You will seek me and find me when you seek me with all your heart." This is not casual seeking. This is a wholehearted pursuit. It means coming to Him not only with our polished prayers, but also with our cracked hearts, our quiet fears, and our hidden wounds. And the reward is not a quick fix—it is a deeper knowledge of who He is and who we are in Him.

When self-doubt creeps in, let prayer be your refuge. Pour out your heart to God, expressing your fears and uncertainties. Then, listen. Allow His Word to speak louder than the lies. Remember, your worth isn't determined by societal standards or personal achievements, but by the unchanging truth that you are His beloved creation.

Romans 10:17 says, *"Faith comes from hearing the message, and the message is heard through the word about Christ."* Every time you open the Word in prayer, your faith is being fed. Your perspective is being recalibrated. And slowly, steadily, the lies lose volume while the truth gains strength.

So, the next time the mirror tries to define you, shift your gaze. Look up. Look in the Word. And look into the eyes of your Maker, who calls you chosen, treasured, and wonderfully made.

*You do not have to feel worthy. You do not have to sound poetic.*
*You just have to come.*
*One step.*
*One breath.*
*One whispered prayer.*

**And He will meet you there.**

# Day 8 Drawing Nearer

1.  In what areas of my life do I struggle to see myself as "fearfully and wonderfully made"?

    _____

    _____

    _____

2.  How can I cultivate faith that believes God's truths over my feelings?

    _____

    _____

    _____

3.  What steps can I take to reinforce my identity in Christ daily?

    _____

    _____

    _____

4.  How can I use prayer to silence self-doubt and speak life over who God says I am?

    _____

    _____

    _____

**Affirmation**

I am fearfully and wonderfully made by God. Through faith, I embrace my identity in Him, rejecting lies and standing firm in His truth.

# Day 8 Prayer

Heavenly Father,

There are days when I forget who I am.
When I stare into the mirror and see failure. Flaws. A woman who just doesn't measure up.
And on those days, I need more than affirmation—I need *truth*.

So today, I quiet the inner critic and listen for You.
You are the One who formed me with purpose, who named me before anyone else had a say.
You are the One who said I am fearfully and wonderfully made—
not accidentally assembled or merely tolerated but *intentionally designed*.

Remind me that my worth is not measured by my performance, my weight, my income, or my title.
It is sealed by the hands that created me and the blood that redeemed me.

Help me unlearn the lies I've believed.
Help me break agreements with insecurity and comparison.
And help me build my identity on the solid foundation of Your Word.

Even when I don't feel beautiful, worthy, or chosen—You say I am.
Even when the world overlooks me—You delight in me.

Teach me to walk in that confidence.
Not with arrogance, but with holy assurance.
I am Yours. And You don't make mistakes.

Thank You for making me on purpose, with purpose.
Let me live today like I believe that's true.

In Jesus' name,
Amen

# Day 9

## WHERE HEALING BEGINS

**Scripture**

Psalm 51:17

*"A broken and contrite heart you, God, will not despise."*

**Focus**

Prayer is where brokenness meets grace and healing begins.

# Day 9 Devotional Reflection

There's a kind of brokenness that feels beyond repair. A deep, aching sorrow over what we've done or what has been done to us that makes us wonder if we're too far gone. But Psalm 51 reminds us that brokenness, when brought to God, is not despised. It is treasured.

David wrote these words after the darkest moral failure of his life. He had sinned. Deeply. Yet, instead of hiding in shame, he turned to God in prayer. Broken. Contrite. Honest. And what did he find? Not rejection. Not wrath. But mercy. David's broken heart didn't push God away. It pulled Him in.

This is the part that wrecks and restores me: two of Jesus' closest followers—Judas and Peter—both failed Him. Judas betrayed Jesus. Peter denied Him. Both felt the weight of guilt. But what they did with that guilt changed everything.

Judas ran from Jesus in isolation. Peter ran toward Jesus in repentance. One allowed shame to become the final chapter. The other let brokenness become the beginning of healing.

Prayer is where that choice is made. When we mess up—because we all do—we have a decision. Will I run and hide? Or will I collapse into the arms of grace? God doesn't ask us to fix ourselves before coming. He asks us to come broken. Because that's the offering He accepts.

This kind of brokenness shows up in everyday life more often than we admit. Maybe it's the mom who snapped at her child and feels the weight of guilt as bedtime approaches. The woman who compromised her boundaries with someone she trusted. The wife who silently regrets words she cannot take back. Or the leader who wonders if she's failed the people looking up to her.

No matter how spiritual we are, we all hit moments that leave us cracked open. And the enemy will always try to shame us into silence. But prayer is where that silence breaks. Prayer is the moment we stop covering and start confessing. It's where healing starts not with perfection, but with presence.

1 John 1:9 assures us, "*If we confess our sins, he is faithful and just and will forgive us our sins and purify us from all unrighteousness.*" Confession is not condemnation. It is cleansing. It is restoration. It is grace in action.

Isaiah 57:15 also echoes this truth: "*I live in a high and holy place, but also with the one who is contrite and lowly in spirit.*" God does not avoid the broken. He moves in. He inhabits the low places with healing, with hope, with holy presence.

Maybe you're carrying something right now. You may be carrying a regret, a secret, or a wound. Bring it to God in prayer. Don't rehearse your guilt. Release it. Don't shrink back in shame. Fall forward into grace. Because what God will not turn away is a heart that's honest, humble, and ready to be made whole.

My friend, maybe today's prayer won't be polished. Maybe it will be messy, tear-stained, raw. That's okay. God isn't put off by the mess. He meets you in it. And He does something only He can do. He holds what's broken and makes it whole.

*You do not have to feel worthy. You do not have to sound poetic.*
*You just have to come.*
*One step.*
*One breath.*
*One whispered prayer.*

**And He will meet you there.**

# Day 9 Drawing Nearer

1. What area of my life feels broken or too far gone—and have I fully brought that to God in prayer?

   _____

   _____

   _____

2. When I feel guilt or shame, do I tend to withdraw like Judas or run toward grace like Peter?

   _____

   _____

   _____

3. How does knowing God welcomes brokenness reshape the way I view my mistakes?

   _____

   _____

   _____

4. What healing might be possible if I offered God my whole heart—even the hurting parts?

   _____

   _____

   _____

**Affirmation**

God meets me in my brokenness and restores me with grace.

# Day 9 Prayer

Lord,

You know what it's like to be broken.
To feel the sting of betrayal. To cry out in grief.
To love people who didn't love You back.
So I trust that You understand the places in me that ache.

I bring You my heartbreak.
The regret I carry, the wounds I hide, the pain I'm still
processing.
I've tried to hold it together for so long,
but You're not asking me to fake it.
You're asking me to bring it.

You said You would never despise a broken and contrite heart.
So here's mine—raw, imperfect, tear-stained, tired.
Here's the part of me I usually keep hidden.

I don't want to just manage the pain—I want to be healed.
I want to be free from the guilt that haunts me.
I want to be whole in the places I've only learned to function
while fractured.

Like David, I fall into Your mercy.
Like Peter, I run back into grace.

And like the woman at the well, I let You speak to the shame I thought would define me forever.

Do what only You can do, God.
Hold me in my brokenness—and begin the healing.

In Jesus' name,
Amen

# Day 10

## ABIDING IN THE VINE

**Scripture**

**John 15:4**

*"Remain in me, as I also remain in you."*

**Focus**

Prayer is the abiding space where connection to God is nurtured.

# Day 10 Devotional Reflection

"Remain." It's such a tender word. Not strive. Not hustle. Just stay. Just be. Jesus invites us into a relationship defined not by effort, but by connection. He is the Vine. We are the branches. And prayer is how we stay tethered.

There's a difference between producing and abiding. One exhausts. The other sustains.

Jesus' invitation in John 15:4 is not to try harder, but to stay closer. He does not ask us to hustle for fruit. He says simply: Remain in Me. Stay connected. Stay rooted. Abide.

For the woman doing all the things—serving, parenting, leading, creating—this word is a holy reset. Because truthfully, we can show up to all the roles and still feel disconnected from the source. We can keep pouring out until there is nothing left in the cup.

Abiding happens in prayer. Not rushed, surface-level prayer, but relationship prayer—the kind that slows us down and reminds us that we are not alone in this. Prayer is not a place to perform. It is where we plug back into the Vine.

Jesus modeled this constantly. He would retreat from the crowds, from the miracles, even from His disciples to pray. Why? Because He knew ministry without intimacy becomes machinery. But intimacy through prayer? That is where the power flows.

Luke 5:16 tells us, *"Jesus often withdrew to lonely places and prayed."* Even the Son of God, filled with purpose and divine mission, needed uninterrupted space to abide. If He made space to remain, how much more should we?

Think of a branch. Its only job is to stay connected to the vine. That connection is what feeds it, strengthens it, causes it to bear fruit. It does not force grapes to grow. It does not strain to bloom. It simply abides, and the vine does the rest.

Galatians 5:22-23 lists the fruit of the Spirit—love, joy, peace, patience, kindness, goodness, faithfulness, gentleness, and self-control. These are not things we can manufacture. They grow as natural evidence of remaining. As we abide, the Spirit produces in us things we cannot produce on our own.

What if today, instead of checking another thing off your list, you stopped and said: God, I just want to be with You. That simple act of abiding might bear more fruit than a thousand good intentions.

*You do not have to feel worthy. You do not have to sound poetic.*
*You just have to come.*
*One step.*
*One breath.*
*One whispered prayer.*

**And He will meet you there.**

# Day 10 Drawing Nearer

1. Where in my life do I feel like I'm producing without truly abiding?

   _____

   _____

   _____

2. What does it look like for me to remain connected to God throughout my day—not just in quiet time, but in the middle of life?

   _____

   _____

   _____

3. What are the signs that I'm living disconnected from the Vine—and how can I respond when I notice them?

   _____

   _____

   _____

4. How can prayer shift from a task to a space of intimate connection with God?

   _____

   _____

   _____

**Affirmation**

I am rooted in Christ. As I remain in Him, He sustains and empowers me.

# Day 10 Prayer

Jesus,

You are the Vine. I am the branch.
And I confess—I've been trying to bear fruit while
disconnected from the Source.
I've been producing, performing, surviving… but not always
*abiding*.

Forgive me for rushing through prayer,
for treating time with You like an item on a list instead of the
air I breathe.
Bring me back to the rhythm of relationship.

I don't want surface-level connection.
I want communion.
I want to stay, not just visit.
I want to rest in You so deeply that fruit becomes the
byproduct of intimacy—not effort.

Teach me how to dwell.
How to linger.
How to build a life that flows *from* You, not just *for* You.

I don't want to run on empty anymore.
Fill me with what only You can supply.
Make my heart a resting place for Your presence.

Because when I abide, I'm never alone.
And when I remain, You remain in me.

Keep me close, Lord.
I never want to be disconnected again.

In Jesus' name,
Amen

# Day 11

## NOTHING CAN SEPARATE

---

**Scripture**

Romans 8:38-39

*"Nothing can separate us from the love of God that is in Christ Jesus our Lord."*

**Focus**

Prayer reminds us of and roots us in His unshakable love.

# Day 11 Devotional Reflection

There are moments when the weight of the world feels overwhelming. When rejection, failure, or loneliness whisper lies that you are unworthy or unloved. In these times, prayer becomes your lifeline, anchoring you to the profound truth of God's unwavering love.

Maybe you are a woman navigating the complexities of modern life—balancing career aspirations, family responsibilities, and personal dreams. You may face moments of self-doubt, questioning your worth or feeling unseen. Yet, in the quiet moments of prayer, you are reminded that God's love is not contingent on your achievements or failures. It is a steadfast, unchanging force that embraces you in every season.

Romans 8:38–39 assures us that nothing—absolutely nothing—can separate us from God's love. Not your past mistakes, present struggles, or future uncertainties. This passage serves as a powerful reminder that God's love is not just a concept but a lived reality, accessible through the intimate act of prayer.

And here's the deeper truth: God does not love you less on your worst day. He does not withdraw when you fall short. His love steps in when your strength runs out. Isaiah 46:4 says, *"Even to your old age and gray hairs I am he, I am he who will sustain you. I have made you and I will carry you; I will sustain you and I will rescue you."* His love is not a reward for your performance. It is a covering, a constant, and a commitment. When you are too weak to rise, His love lifts. When you are too broken to believe, His love holds. He assures you not just with words but with presence. He will love you through it. Nurture you through it. Bring you through it.

In prayer, you find a sacred space to lay down your burdens, to voice your fears, and to bask in the assurance of being deeply loved. It is where your heart realigns with the truth that you are cherished, not because of what you do, but because of who you are in Christ.

Let's bring it closer to home. Maybe you are the woman who poured yourself into a relationship that did not last, and now you are left questioning your worth. Or perhaps you are the mom who feels invisible, wondering if anyone sees the sacrifices you make daily. Maybe you are the professional who has hit a wall, feeling like your best efforts are not enough. In all these scenarios, prayer is the space where God gently whispers, "You are mine. You are loved beyond measure."

Prayer does not require you to have it all together. It invites you to come as you are—messy, broken, and real. It is in this honest communion that you experience the depth of God's love, a love that heals wounds, restores hope, and reaffirms your identity in Him.

*You do not have to feel worthy. You do not have to sound poetic.*
*You just have to come.*
*One step.*
*One breath.*
*One whispered prayer.*

**And He will meet you there.**

# Day 11 Drawing Nearer

1. In what areas of my life have I doubted God's love for me?

   _____

   _____

   _____

2. How can I use prayer to reinforce the truth of God's unshakable love in my daily life?

   _____

   _____

   _____

3. Reflect on a time when you felt distant from God. How did you reconnect with His love?

   _____

   _____

   _____

4. What practical steps can I take to remind myself of God's love during challenging times?

   _____

   _____

   _____

**Affirmation**

God's love surrounds me. Nothing can separate me from Him—not ever.

# Day 11 Prayer

Heavenly Father,

Sometimes I feel distant—not because You moved,
but because life distracted me, disappointment disoriented me,
or shame tried to silence me.
But Your Word says that nothing can separate me from Your
love.

Not my past.
Not my present.
Not what I've done.
Not what's been done to me.

Your love is not fragile.
It doesn't waver with my mood swings or shrink when I make
mistakes.
It's steady. Unshakable. Everlasting.

So today I come boldly—not because I've earned anything,
but because Jesus already paid for everything.

Wrap me in the truth of Your love.
Help me to stop second-guessing if You're still here.
Remind me that I'm not on probation—I'm already accepted.

I'm not an outsider—I'm a daughter.
Chosen. Wanted. Safe.

Let that truth saturate my mind, my emotions, and my decisions.
And when doubt creeps in again, let me remember that the cross already proved Your answer:
You. Will. Not. Let. Me. Go.

I am forever held.
And I am forever loved.

In Jesus' name,
Amen

# Day 12

## SEEING WITH A PURE HEART

---

**Scripture**

Matthew 5:8

*"Blessed are the pure in heart, for they will see God."*

**Focus**

Prayer purifies and sensitizes our hearts to His presence.

# Day 12 Devotional Reflection

There's something sacred about a heart that longs to be clean. Not polished for appearances but purified for intimacy. David's cry in Psalm 51:10 wasn't about image management. It was a desperate plea for restoration. He knew that sin dulled his sensitivity to God's presence, and he yearned for that connection to be restored.

Prayer is the space where this purification happens. It is where we lay bare our hearts, allowing God to cleanse the clutter and noise that distract us from His voice. As we confess and surrender, He renews our spirit and makes us more attuned to His presence in our daily lives.

Think about the times when life feels overwhelming. When the demands of work, family, and personal struggles cloud your spiritual vision. In those moments, prayer becomes your sanctuary. It is where you recalibrate, shedding the weight of the world and embracing the peace that comes from being in God's presence.

Maybe you are the woman who starts her day in a whirlwind of tasks, barely catching your breath. But then in a quiet moment of prayer—just five minutes before anyone else wakes up—you find clarity and strength. Your heart, once burdened, becomes sensitive again to the gentle nudges of the Holy Spirit, guiding your steps and decisions.

This sensitivity is not about emotionalism. It is about alignment. As your heart is purified through prayer, you become more receptive to God's guidance, more aware of His movements in your life. You begin to see His fingerprints in the mundane and hear His whispers amidst the chaos.

Jesus exemplified this in His ministry. He often withdrew to solitary places to pray, not out of obligation, but to maintain an unbroken connection with the Father. His sensitivity to God's presence empowered Him to act with compassion, wisdom, and authority. In the same way, your times of prayer refine your heart and enable you to live and love more like Him.

And here is the part that might just hit a little deeper: a pure heart is not a perfect one. It is a surrendered one. God is not asking you to present a flawless soul, only an available one. Psalm 24:3–4 says, "*Who may stand in His holy place? The one who has clean hands and a pure heart.*" That place of holiness is not earned. It is entered through honesty, humility, and hunger. The more you pray, the more He purifies. And the more He purifies, the more clearly you begin to see Him—not just in your quiet time, but in the chaos, the choices, and the calling.

*You do not have to feel worthy. You do not have to sound poetic.*
*You just have to come.*
*One step.*
*One breath.*
*One whispered prayer.*

**And He will meet you there.**

# Day 12 Drawing Nearer

1. What areas of my heart need purification to better sense God's presence?

   _____

   _____

   _____

2. How does regular prayer help me stay attuned to the Holy Spirit's guidance?

   _____

   _____

   _____

3. Reflect on a time when prayer brought clarity or peace in a chaotic situation.

   _____

   _____

   _____

4. What steps can I take to create a daily rhythm of prayer that fosters sensitivity to God?

   _____

   _____

   _____

**Affirmation**

My heart is open and pure before God—I see Him, I know Him, and I reflect His beauty.

# Day 12 Prayer

Lord,

I want to see You—not just with my eyes, but with my heart.
But sometimes my vision is clouded.
By bitterness. By fear. By disappointment. By distraction.

So today, I pray like David:
Create in me a clean heart, O God.
Renew a right spirit within me.
Wash away the residue of old wounds and current worries.
Clear the clutter so I can perceive You more clearly.

Make my heart soft again.
Sensitive to Your Spirit.
Attuned to Your whisper.
Free from judgment, pride, and spiritual numbness.

I want to see You in the mundane
In the eyes of my children.
In the sunlight through the window.
In the unexpected kindness of a stranger.
Help me to recognize You where I once overlooked You.

Let my purity not be performance,
but the fruit of proximity.
As I spend time with You, make me more like You.

I want to see You.
And I want to reflect You.

In Jesus' name,
Amen

# Day 13

## A THIRST ONLY HE CAN QUENCH

**Scripture**

Psalm 63:1

*"You, God, are my God, earnestly I seek you… my soul thirsts for you."*

**Focus**

Prayer quenches the soul's longing for intimacy with God.

# Day 13 Devotional Reflection

There's a thirst that no amount of success, relationships, or self-care can satisfy. A longing so deep it echoes through our souls. David knew this thirst intimately. In Psalm 63:1, penned during his time in the wilderness of Judah, he writes, "*You, God, are my God, earnestly I seek you; my soul thirsts for you.*" Despite the physical desolation surrounding him, David's deepest yearning was for the presence of God.

This kind of thirst is not quenched by the temporary comforts of life. It is a spiritual craving for connection, purpose, and love that only God can fulfill. Prayer becomes the wellspring where this thirst is met—not with mere drops, but with a deluge of His presence. As we pour out our hearts, God pours in His peace, love, and affirmation.

Maybe you are the woman juggling the demands of a career, family, and personal aspirations. Your calendar is full, but your soul feels dry. You wake up early, stay up late, meet everyone else's needs—and yet something inside still aches. That ache is not weakness. It is an invitation. In the quiet moments of prayer, you reconnect with the source of your strength and remember that your deepest needs are met not by doing more, but by being still in God's presence.

Jesus spoke of this thirst in John 4:13–14, telling the Samaritan woman at the well that whoever drinks the water He gives will never thirst again. This living water becomes a spring within, welling up to eternal life. Prayer is the vessel through which we receive this living water, refreshing our souls and aligning our desires with His.

In our modern wildernesses—whether stress, loneliness, loss, or the constant pursuit of meaning—prayer remains the oasis where our souls are revived. It is not about eloquent words or perfect settings. It is about an earnest heart seeking the One who satisfies. As we draw near to God in prayer, we find that our thirst leads us not to despair, but to the depths of His love and grace.

And here is the beauty of it all: God does not shame you for being thirsty. He invites it. Psalm 107:9 says, *"He satisfies the thirsty and fills the hungry with good things."* Your longing is not a liability. It is the very place where God desires to meet you. He will not hand you a cup and ask you to ration it. He will flood your soul with more than you knew you needed. The wilderness may be dry, but the well never is.

*You do not have to feel worthy. You do not have to sound poetic. You just have to come.*

*One step.*
*One breath.*
*One whispered prayer.*

**And He will meet you there.**

# Day 13 Drawing Nearer

1. What areas of my life feel spiritually dry, and how can I bring them to God in prayer?

   _____

   _____

   _____

2. In what ways have I tried to quench my soul's thirst with things other than God's presence?

   _____

   _____

   _____

3. How does acknowledging my spiritual thirst draw me closer to God?

   _____

   _____

   _____

4. What steps can I take to cultivate a deeper intimacy with God through prayer?

   _____

   _____

   _____

**Affirmation**

My soul thirsts for God, and He faithfully satisfies me with His presence.

# Day 13 Prayer

Lord,

I'm thirsty—not physically, but spiritually.
There's an ache in me that no relationship, achievement, or vacation can satisfy.
It's deeper than exhaustion. It's longing.
And You're the only One who can meet it.

Like a thirsty soul in the desert, I long for You.
Not just for what You can do, but for who You are.
I don't want shallow sips—I want to drink deeply from Your presence.

Forgive me for trying to quench that thirst with everything else.
For numbing with entertainment.
For chasing distraction.
For filling my schedule instead of filling my spirit.

Draw me back to the well that never runs dry.
Back to the quiet place.
Back to the waters of refreshment that come only from time spent with You.

Satisfy my soul, God.
Saturate the dry places.

Flood the cracks in my confidence.
Drench the parts of me that have forgotten how to hope.

I don't just want to survive.
I want to be *renewed.*

Let Your presence be my drink of living water.
Again and again.

In Jesus' name,
Amen

# Day 14

## REFLECTING HIS GLORY

---

**Scripture**

2 Corinthians 3:18

*"And we all… are being transformed into his image with ever-increasing glory."*

**Focus**

Prayer is a place of transformation and reflection of His glory.

# Day 14 Devotional Reflection

There's a sacred mystery in the way God meets us in prayer—not just to hear our hearts, but to reshape them. In 2 Corinthians 3:18, Paul speaks of a transformation that occurs when we behold the Lord's glory. This transformation is not a one-time event. It is an ongoing process, a journey from one degree of glory to another, orchestrated by the Spirit.

Imagine standing in front of a mirror that does not simply reflect your image but begins to refine it. That is what happens when we spend time in the presence of God. Our hearts, attitudes, and even our desires begin to shift. We begin to reflect His character—His patience, His peace, His compassion, and His strength. This is not about striving to be better. It is about surrendering to the One who makes us new from the inside out.

Maybe you are a woman stepping into something unfamiliar, a new business, a big vision, a bold calling. You have poured your heart into it, but the uncertainty still looms large. Will this succeed? Can I really do this? What if I fail? You might be tempted to throw yourself into nonstop effort, measuring progress by productivity and scrolling social media for validation. But the truth is, no spreadsheet or strategy can bring the soul-deep transformation your spirit craves. Only God can do that.

When you turn to prayer, everything begins to shift. You enter a sacred space where your fears are calmed, your motives are purified, and your identity is clarified—not as a brand builder or role filler, but as a beloved daughter of the King. That truth grounds you. In prayer, you remember that your value is not tied to metrics or milestones. It is rooted in grace. And in that grace, you find the power to show up, not from pressure, but from peace.

Romans 12:2 reinforces this by saying, *"Do not conform to the pattern of this world, but be transformed by the renewing of your mind."* That renewal happens in prayer. It is where God peels away the layers of fear and comparison and reveals the version of you that He sees. The version full of purpose, filled with love, and anchored in truth. This is not a transformation you have to force. It is one you receive.

And this change is not just for you. As you are transformed, you become a mirror that reflects God's glory into the lives of others. Your words carry healing. Your posture carries humility. Your actions invite others to wonder what it is that makes you different. And that wonder leads to witness. The transformation God works in you becomes a testimony for the world.

So then, approach prayer not as a duty or a checkbox, but as a divine invitation to transformation. You are not just coming to be heard. You are coming to be changed.

*You do not have to feel worthy. You do not have to sound poetic.*
*You just have to come.*
*One step.*
*One breath.*
*One whispered prayer.*

**And He will meet you there.**

# Day 14 Drawing Nearer

1. In what areas of my life do I sense God is calling me to deeper transformation?

   _____

   _____

   _____

2. How does spending time in prayer change my perspective on daily challenges?

   _____

   _____

   _____

3. Reflect on a moment when you felt God's presence deeply during prayer. What changed in you as a result?

   _____

   _____

   _____

4. How can I intentionally make space for transformative encounters with God in my daily routine?

   _____

   _____

   _____

**Affirmation**

As I gaze upon God, I am transformed by His glory—day by day, step by step.

# Day 14 Prayer

Lord,

Your Word says we are being transformed into Your image with ever-increasing glory.
But some days, I don't feel like I'm reflecting anything but stress, doubt, or fatigue.
So today, I come not to pretend—but to be transformed.

Shape me in Your presence.
Let time with You sand down what's sharp in me.
Refine what's rough. Heal what's hurting.
And polish what still feels too dim to shine.

I don't want to be a mirror for culture.
I want to reflect *Christ*.

Change how I respond under pressure.
Change how I love when it's hard.
Change how I show up when no one's watching.

Let my life reveal You—
In how I speak, how I serve, how I suffer, and how I lead.
Not for applause, but for glory.
Not for perfection, but for transformation.

Do the deep work in me, Lord.

So when others see me, they catch a glimpse of *You.*

In Jesus' name,

Amen

# Day 15

## DEEPER UNION WITH CHRIST

**Scripture**

Philippians 3:10

*"I want to know Christ—yes, to know the power of his resurrection and participation in his sufferings."*

**Focus**

Prayer is one way we pursue deeper knowing and union with Christ.

# Day 15 Devotional Reflection

In the whirlwind of our daily lives, it's easy to settle for a surface-level relationship with Christ. We check off devotionals, attend church, and say quick prayers. But deep down, there is a yearning for more and a desire not just to know about Jesus, but to truly know Him. To experience an intimate union that transforms us from the inside out.

The Apostle Paul captures this longing in Philippians 3:10. He expresses a desire to know Christ intimately, to share in both His resurrection power and His sufferings. This is not a casual acquaintance. It is a deep, abiding relationship that touches every corner of our lives and redefines who we are from the inside out.

Maybe you are a woman juggling the demands of a career, raising a family, and chasing personal dreams. Your days are full, your plate is heavy, and on the outside, everything looks functional. But deep within, you know your soul is craving more than routine. You long for something deeper than Christian checklists and spiritual performance. You ache for communion with Christ that brings peace amidst chaos, clarity in confusion, and purpose in the midst of the mundane.

Prayer becomes that place. Your sacred refuge. Not the rushed kind you whisper while multitasking, but the kind that stops time and opens the soul. In that quiet space, you lay down the weight of expectations and breathe in the presence of your Savior. You do not come to impress Him. You come to know Him. And in doing so, something inside you begins to shift. Your prayers become conversations. Your silence becomes sacred. Your faith becomes friendship.

This journey toward deeper union with Christ is not always smooth. It will ask something of you. It requires intentional time, inner honesty, and a willingness to walk with Him through both celebration and suffering. But it also comes with an unmatched reward—intimacy with the Living God. It is not always loud, but it is always life-giving.

John 15:15 offers a beautiful reminder of Jesus' heart toward this kind of relationship: "*I no longer call you servants... Instead, I have called you friends.*" Imagine that. The Son of God inviting you into friendship, not just formality. That kind of relationship does not develop overnight. It grows in the soil of consistency, trust, and vulnerability. And prayer is where it takes root.

As you continue to seek Him through prayer, you discover a love that does not waver, a voice that speaks even when you are weary, and a strength that holds you through every season.

Knowing Christ is not about religion. Knowing Christ is about relationship. It is about waking up each day and choosing Him over everything else the world offers

So let us also pursue this deeper union. Let prayer be more than a discipline. Let it be a doorway. The bridge that connects our hearts to His. And in doing so, we open ourselves to a relationship that transforms, renews, and empowers us to live fully in His grace.

*You do not have to feel worthy. You do not have to sound poetic.*
*You just have to come.*
*One step.*
*One breath.*
*One whispered prayer.*

**And He will meet you there.**

# Day 15 Drawing Nearer

1.  In what areas of my life do I sense God is calling me to deeper intimacy with Him?

   _____

   _____

   _____

2.  How can I create intentional space in my daily routine to connect with Christ through prayer?

   _____

   _____

   _____

3.  Reflect on a time when prayer led you to a deeper understanding of God's love. What changed in you as a result?

   _____

   _____

   _____

4.  What steps can I take to cultivate a more profound communion with Christ amidst the busyness of life?

   _____

   _____

   _____

**Affirmation**

I seek to know Christ deeply—in every joy, in every sorrow, and in all things in between.

# Day 15 Prayer

Heavenly Father,

I don't want a surface-level relationship with You.
I don't want to know facts about You but miss Your presence.
I don't want to go through religious motions and still feel
empty inside.

I want to *know* You. Deeply. Intimately. Personally.
To walk with You not just on Sunday mornings, but on messy
Mondays.
To invite You into the moments I'm most tempted to hide.
To lean on You when life shakes me—and even when it
doesn't.

Like Paul, I want to know the power of Your resurrection,
but I also want to learn from the weight of Your suffering.
To find You not just in the miracles, but in the mundane.
Not just in the joy, but in the ache.

Pull me closer, Lord.
Not because I deserve it—but because You desire it.

Unify my heart with Yours.
Let me feel what moves You.
Let me desire what pleases You.

Let me obey not out of obligation, but out of deep, unshakeable love.

And when I'm tempted to pull away—draw me back.
Let me be so anchored in You that no storm, no success, no struggle can separate us.

More than anything this world can offer,
I just want *You.*

In Jesus' name,
Amen

# Day 16

## A NEW HEART WITHIN

**Scripture**

Ezekiel 36:26

*"I will give you a new heart and put a new spirit in you."*

**Focus**

Prayer positions us to receive God's renewing work within.

# Day 16 Devotional Reflection

There are seasons when our spiritual fervor wanes. Not out of defiance, but perhaps due to the slow fade of complacency. We find ourselves going through the motions. Our prayers become mechanical. Our worship routine. The vibrant relationship we once cherished with God feels distant, and our hearts grow cold, unresponsive to His gentle nudges.

Ezekiel 36:26 speaks directly into this state: "*I will give you a new heart and put a new spirit in you.*" This isn't a one-time offer but a continual invitation to transformation. God doesn't merely patch up our weary hearts; He replaces them, breathing new life into our spirits. Through sincere, honest prayer, we position ourselves to receive this divine renewal.

Maybe you are a woman who once burned with passion for God, but lately you feel disconnected. You still believe, but something feels dull. Flat. Numb. You try to read your Bible, but the words feel distant. You show up to church, but your spirit feels dry. That vibrant fire you once carried has dimmed. And maybe, deep down, you feel guilty about it. But friend, God is not disappointed in your weariness. He is drawing near to you in it. He is not asking you to manufacture a new flame. He is offering to breathe life into the embers.

In prayer, you do not have to pretend. You simply have to be present. It may sound like, "God, I feel nothing, but I want to feel You again." Or "God, I don't know where the fire went, but I miss it." And that honesty is enough to unlock the beginning of renewal. Because the God who promised a new heart is not waiting for you to fix the old one. He is waiting for you to surrender it.

Imagine what happens when you bring that tired, stony heart into His presence. You are not met with shame. You are met with softness. A tenderness that starts to peel away the layers of bitterness, distraction, or exhaustion. And slowly, something begins to pulse again. You begin to hunger. To hope. To feel.

Let us remember that God's offer of a new heart and spirit is not limited to our initial conversion. It is a perpetual promise, available whenever we find ourselves in need of His renewing touch. Through prayer, we open the door for God to do His transformative work within us, restoring our passion, realigning our desires, and rekindling our love for Him.

*You do not have to feel worthy. You do not have to sound poetic.*
*You just have to come.*
*One step.*

*One breath.*
*One whispered prayer.*

**And He will meet you there.**

# Day 16 Drawing Nearer

1. Are there areas in my life where I've grown spiritually complacent?

   _____

   _____

   _____

2. What steps can I take to rekindle my passion for God?

   _____

   _____

   _____

3. How has God renewed my heart in the past, and what did that transformation look like?

   _____

   _____

   _____

4. In what ways can I position myself through prayer to receive God's renewing work today?

   _____

   _____

   _____

**Affirmation**

God is renewing my heart and restoring my spirit—fresh, faithful, and full of life.

# Day 16 Prayer

Father,

You said You would give me a new heart and put a new spirit within me.
And Lord, I need that today.
Because some days, this heart feels weary. Hardened.
Unresponsive to things that used to stir me.
Distracted when I long to be present.
Numb when I want to feel deeply.

So I'm asking You—do heart surgery on me, God.
Take what's calloused and make it soft again.
Remove what's heavy and breathe fresh life where there's been dryness.

I don't want to settle for going through the motions.
I want to be fully alive to You.
Fully surrendered. Fully present. Fully in love with the One who's never stopped loving me.

Renew my spirit.
Let joy return where fatigue has taken over.
Let conviction rise where I've been complacent.
Let compassion reign where I've grown impatient or indifferent.

You're not just trying to improve me—you're transforming me.
You're making me new from the inside out.

So do what only You can do.
Make this heart beat like Yours again.

In your precious name,
Amen

# Day 17

## TRUSTING THE GUIDE

---

**Scripture**

Proverbs 3:5–6

*"Trust in the Lord with all your heart… and he will make your paths straight."*

**Focus**

Prayer helps us surrender control and trust His guidance.

# Day 17 Devotional Reflection

There are moments in life when the ground beneath us seems to shift, and the path ahead becomes obscured by uncertainty. For a woman facing a severe health crisis, each day can feel like navigating through a dense fog, where familiar landmarks of routine and normalcy have vanished. The diagnosis, the treatments, the waiting—all contribute to a sense of helplessness and a longing for clarity.

In these moments, Proverbs 3:5–6 becomes more than just a comforting verse. It transforms into a lifeline. Trusting in the Lord with all our heart means releasing our grip on the need to understand every detail of our journey. It calls us to surrender our fears, our questions, and our desire for control, placing them into the hands of a God who sees the entire picture.

Prayer becomes the conduit through which this trust is both expressed and strengthened. It is in the quiet moments of honest conversation with God that we find the courage to face another day. Through prayer, we acknowledge our limitations and invite God's infinite wisdom to guide us. We may not receive immediate answers, but we gain the assurance that we are not alone—that our paths are being directed by a loving and sovereign God.

Maybe you are a woman walking through a health battle right now. You wake up every day with questions that do not have clear answers. You might feel like your body is failing and your faith is flickering. But you keep showing up in prayer. Not because you have all the right words, but because you know the One who holds the unknown. Every whispered cry, every tear you do not even speak aloud, is heard by a God who promises to lead you, even when the way is hidden.

Trust is not passive. It is not silence in the storm. It is the active, radical decision to hand your fears to God day after day. Isaiah 26:3 reminds us, *"You will keep in perfect peace those whose minds are steadfast, because they trust in you."* That peace does not come from understanding. It comes from trusting the One who does.

And here is the grace that hits different: God does not expect you to carry this trust on your own. He supplies it. He builds it in you as you pray, as you wait, as you weep, as you worship. Psalm 32:8 says, *"I will instruct you and teach you in the way you should go; I will counsel you with my loving eye on you."* He is not a distant God pointing to a path. He is right beside you, guiding with love.

This trust does not eliminate the pain or the struggle, but it infuses them with purpose and hope. It reminds us that even in our darkest hours, God is at work, directing our paths toward healing, growth, and deeper intimacy with Him.

*You do not have to feel worthy. You do not have to sound poetic.*
*You just have to come.*
*One step.*
*One breath.*
*One whispered prayer.*

**And He will meet you there.**

# Day 17 Drawing Nearer

1. What fears or uncertainties am I holding onto that I need to surrender to God?

   _____

   _____

   _____

2. How has God guided me through past challenges, and how can that encourage me now?

   _____

   _____

   _____

3. In what ways can I cultivate a deeper trust in God's plan for my life, especially during trials?

   _____

   _____

   _____

4. How can I support others who are facing their own health crises, pointing them toward trust in the Lord?

   _____

   _____

   _____

**Affirmation**

I trust God with my whole heart—He is guiding my path, and I will follow.

# Day 17 Prayer

Lord,

Sometimes life feels like a maze.
So many decisions. So much uncertainty.
And deep down, I want to trust You—but I still find myself
trying to map my own path.

You said to trust You with all my heart,
to lean not on my own understanding,
and that You would make my paths straight.

So today, I let go of the illusion of control.
I surrender my timeline.
My backup plans.
My carefully constructed "what ifs."

You are the God who sees beyond what I see.
Who knows the road I haven't walked yet.
Who gently guides, even when I feel lost or unsure.

Help me to trust You—not just in theory, but in practice.
Help me to believe that even when I don't understand the
detour, You are still directing my steps.
And when fear tries to creep in, let Your voice grow louder
than my doubt.

You are my Guide. My Shepherd.
My trusted Navigator.

I will follow—even if I can't yet see where we're going.
Because You've never led me anywhere Your grace hasn't
already gone before me.

In Jesus' name,
Amen

# Day 18

## A HIGHER PERSPECTIVE

**Scripture**

Colossians 3:2

*"Set your minds on things above, not on earthly things."*

**Focus**

Prayer lifts our perspective and resets our spiritual focus.

# Day 18 Devotional Reflection

Life is a series of seasons, each bringing its own set of challenges and opportunities. For many women, entering a new season—such as becoming an empty nester or stepping into retirement—can be both liberating and disorienting. The roles that once defined daily life shift, leaving a void that is both tangible and emotional.

In these moments, Colossians 3:2 serves as a gentle reminder to redirect our focus. *"Set your minds on things above, not on earthly things."* It is more than a mindset shift. It is an invitation to lift our gaze from the shifting ground beneath us to the solid, eternal truths that anchor our faith.

Prayer becomes the bridge between our current reality and God's divine perspective. Through intentional time in His presence, we can realign our thoughts, release our fears, and allow His peace to settle in our hearts. This does not erase the ache of transition or the questions that come with it, but it gives us something stronger to hold onto. Prayer steadies us when our sense of identity is being rewritten.

Maybe you are a woman who has recently retired after decades of dedicated work. Your calendar looks different now. The structure that once gave your day rhythm is suddenly gone, and with it, some of the sense of purpose you once carried. In prayer, you begin bringing your uncertainty to God. Not with polished words, but with honest questions. And over time, you start to see what He's unfolding. Maybe you begin mentoring younger women, volunteering where your voice and wisdom make impact, or finally writing the book that's been sitting on your heart. Your prayers shift your focus—not just to what has ended, but to what God is beginning.

Maybe you are a mother adjusting to the silence of an empty home. The energy, the movement, the noise—it is all quieter now. And with that quiet, unexpected grief rises up. But in prayer, something beautiful happens. God meets you in the stillness. He reminds you that you are not just a mom missing the chaos of motherhood. You are a cherished daughter with a calling that still matters. A woman with time, wisdom, and gifts that are just beginning to bloom in this new season.

Isaiah 43:19 offers this promise: *"See, I am doing a new thing! Now it springs up; do you not perceive it?"* But sometimes, we miss the new thing because we are so focused on what we lost. Prayer is what sharpens our spiritual vision. It helps us perceive what God is planting, even before it takes root.

These transitions, while difficult, are holy ground. They are sacred invitations to grow, to shift, and to receive something new. By setting our minds on things above, we are not escaping reality.  Instead, we are reinterpreting it through the lens of eternity. We are choosing to see with kingdom eyes instead of earthly fear.

So today, if you are in between seasons, feeling a little lost or unsure, bring it all into the presence of God. Let prayer reframe your perspective. Let it remind you that you are not behind. You are being led forward by a God who always knows the next chapter.

*You do not have to feel worthy. You do not have to sound poetic.*
*You just have to come.*
*One step.*
*One breath.*
*One whispered prayer.*

**And He will meet you there.**

# Day 18 Drawing Nearer

1.  What emotions am I experiencing in this new season of life?

    _____

    _____

    _____

2.  How can I intentionally set my mind on things above during this transition?

    _____

    _____

    _____

3.  What new opportunities might God be revealing to me in this season?

    _____

    _____

    _____

4.  How can I use prayer to navigate the uncertainties and embrace the possibilities ahead?

    _____

    _____

    _____

**Affirmation**

My mind is set on things above—my spirit is lifted, and my heart is aligned with heaven.

# Day 18 Prayer

Heavenly Father,

Lift my eyes.
Because sometimes all I can see is what's right in front of me—
the stress, the bills, the tension, the waiting.
But You've called me to set my mind on things above.

So today, I ask You to elevate my vision.
Help me zoom out and see with eternity in mind.
Help me remember that my identity isn't tied to this season.
That my worth isn't attached to productivity or performance.
That my calling isn't over just because something familiar has
ended.

Give me a glimpse of what You're doing behind the scenes.
A sense of Your purpose in what feels pointless.
Remind me that nothing is wasted when it's surrendered to
You.
That You still bring beauty from dust, and clarity from
confusion.
That You are not done writing my story.

Let my mind dwell not on fear, but on faith.
Not on lack, but on Your abundance.

Not on what's broken, but on the One who restores.
Not on what I've lost, but on all I've gained in You.

Reset my focus, God.
Anchor my thoughts in truth.
Shape my perspective, not by my circumstances, but by Your sovereignty.
And when I forget—when my thoughts wander and my hope feels thin—
Draw me back again. Steady me again.

Help me live today with heaven on my mind.

In Jesus' name,
Amen

# Day 19

## LONGING FOR LIVING WATER

**Scripture**

Psalm 42:1–2

*"As the deer pants for streams of water, so my soul pants for you, my God. My soul thirsts for God, for the living God."*

**Focus**

Prayer expresses and fulfills our deep longing for God.

# Day 19 Devotional Reflection

There's something sacred about longing. It means your soul remembers where it came from—and where it belongs. David paints such a vivid picture here: a deer desperate for water, driven by instinct and survival. That's how our souls long for God—whether we realize it or not.

Prayer is the response to that holy thirst. It's not a ritual. It's a cry. A reaching. A recognition that no amount of busyness, success, or comfort will satisfy the deep ache inside. Only the presence of the Living God can do that.

And the beauty is, He always answers that longing. Not with guilt. Not with delay. But with Himself. So do not ignore your thirst today. Honor it. Let it lead you into the arms of the One who quenches it forever.

Yet, in our daily lives, it is easy to misinterpret this spiritual thirst. We might attempt to satisfy it with achievements, relationships, or material possessions, only to find ourselves still yearning. This persistent emptiness is not failure. It is a gentle nudge from our soul, reminding us that only God can truly satisfy our deepest desires.

Maybe you are a woman who seems to have it all together. You have the career, the kids, the calendar full of responsibilities and events. Yet there is this quiet emptiness you cannot explain. You do not feel sad exactly. Just hollow. And maybe even a little guilty for feeling that way. But here's the truth: your soul is not broken. It's thirsty. And that longing is not a weakness. It is your lifeline.

You go to prayer. Not with a to-do list or a performance script, but with your hands open and your heart exposed. You whisper, "God, I don't even know what I need. I just know it's You." And in that moment, something sacred unfolds. His presence meets your ache. His peace quiets the ache. His love begins to fill the cracks.

Jesus said in John 7:37, "*Let anyone who is thirsty come to me and drink.*" That invitation still stands. There is no shame in being thirsty. The danger is in pretending you are not. The most powerful prayers often start with the simplest truth: *I need You, God. I miss You. I want more of You.*

Let us, too, embrace our spiritual thirst as a divine invitation. Through sincere and consistent prayer, we draw closer to God, allowing Him to fill every void and heal every wound. In His presence, our souls find the refreshment and satisfaction they have been longing for.

And when you start to feel dry again—because we all do—do not judge yourself. Just return to the well. Return to the Word. Return to prayer. Because the Living Water never runs out.

*You do not have to feel worthy. You do not have to sound poetic.*
*You just have to come.*
*One step.*
*One breath.*
*One whispered prayer.*

**And He will meet you there.**

# Day 19 Drawing Nearer

1. What areas of my life have I tried to satisfy with worldly things instead of seeking God?

_____

_____

_____

2. How does acknowledging my spiritual thirst change the way I approach prayer?

_____

_____

_____

3. Reflect on a time when God's presence brought you peace amidst chaos. What did you learn from that experience?

_____

_____

_____

4. What steps can I take to cultivate a deeper longing for God in my daily routine?

_____

_____

_____

**Affirmation**

My soul's deepest longing is fulfilled in God's presence.
Through prayer, I am continually refreshed and satisfied by His unending love.

# Day 19 Prayer

Lord,

My soul is thirsty—and You are the only One who can satisfy.
I've tried to fill the ache with things that don't last.
Success. Approval. Distraction.
But the thirst always returns.

You said that if I come to You, I'll never thirst again.
Not because life gets easier—but because *You* become enough.
So I'm coming now. Weary. Thirsty. Open. Ready.

Pour out the living water of Your Spirit.
Saturate the dry, depleted places in me.
Fill every crack with comfort.
Every ache with assurance.
Every longing with Your love.

Remind me that I don't have to be perfect to be filled—just
present.
And that Your presence is the well that never runs dry.

Let my thirst lead me to worship.
Let my longing become intimacy.
Let every part of me that craves be met by the One who created
me to crave *You.*

Today, I drink deeply.
And I am satisfied.

In Jesus' name,
Amen

# Day 20

## LIVING FROM THE INSIDE OUT

**Scripture**

Galatians 2:20

*"I have been crucified with Christ, and I no longer live, but Christ lives in me…"*

**Focus:**

Prayer is how we align ourselves with God's truth and live it out daily.

# Day 20 Devotional Reflection

There are moments when the whispers of self-doubt grow loud, telling us we're not enough, that our past defines us, or that we're unworthy of God's love. These lies can take root, especially when we face challenges, when life feels fragile, or when the world's standards seem impossibly high. Shame becomes a shadow, following us into every room, every relationship, every opportunity.

But Galatians 2:20 offers a powerful truth: our old selves, with all their insecurities, sins, failures, and fears, have been crucified with Christ. That means they no longer get the final word. That means your story is not defined by who you used to be, but by who lives in you now. Christ lives in you. And where Christ lives, shame cannot stay.

Prayer becomes the bridge between these truths and our daily experiences. Through prayer, we can confront the lies we've believed, replacing them with God's promises. In prayer, we do more than vent or ask. We exchange. We hand over unworthy thoughts and pick up the holy truth. We say, "God, I feel small," and He reminds us, "You are mine." We say, "I've failed," and He whispers, "But I've forgiven."

Maybe you are a woman who has been carrying a sense of unworthiness for years. A mistake from your past haunts your present. You smile on the outside, but deep down, you wonder if God really wants to use someone like you. In prayer, you finally bring it to Him. The guilt. The fear. The shame. And He doesn't turn away. He meets you there with grace. He reminds you that what you thought disqualified you is the very place where He wants to show His redemption. You begin to walk differently. Not perfectly, but boldly. Because now you remember who lives in you.

This is the power of crucified living. It is not a life of defeat or self-hatred. It is a life of surrender and spiritual authority. When you fully grasp that Christ lives in you, you stop performing and start abiding. You stop striving and start standing in confidence. And that confidence is not pride. It is identity.

Romans 8:1 says, "Therefore, there is now no condemnation for those who are in Christ Jesus." That is not a future promise. It is a right-now reality. You are not condemned. You are not disqualified. You are not defined by your past. You are alive in Christ. And that changes everything.

Let us, too, embrace this truth daily. Through prayer, we can silence the lies, reaffirm our identity in Christ, and live out the abundant life He offers. Every time we pray, we are saying yes to grace and no to guilt. We are choosing truth over trauma, freedom over fear, and Christ over everything else.

*You do not have to feel worthy. You do not have to sound poetic.*
*You just have to come.*
*One step.*
*One breath.*
*One whispered prayer.*

**And He will meet you there.**

# Day 20 Drawing Nearer

1. What lies have I believed about myself that contradict God's truth?

   _____

   _____

   _____

2. How can I use prayer to reaffirm my identity in Christ daily?

   _____

   _____

   _____

3. In what areas of my life do I need to replace self-doubt with God's promises?

   _____

   _____

   _____

4. How can I support other women in embracing their identity in Christ?

   _____

   _____

   _____

**Affirmation**

I am a new creation in Christ. Through prayer, I align with God's truth, silencing self-doubt and embracing His purpose for my life.

# Day 20 Prayer

Lord,

The world tells me to curate the outside—
the image, the brand, the highlight reel.
But You care about what's within.

You look past the filters and see the fears.
Past the perfection and see the pressure.
And You say, *Live from the inside out.*

So, I invite You in—
into the heartache, the hidden places, the stories I don't tell.
Into the mess, the miracle, and the in-between.

Let my identity be rooted in Christ, not culture.
Let Your Spirit reshape my thoughts, my desires, my default
settings.

I don't want to build a life that looks good but feels hollow.
I want a soul that's aligned with heaven,
a spirit that overflows with Your truth,
a life that reflects what's happening in the secret place.

Change me at the core, God.
And let everything else flow from there.

In Jesus' name,
Amen

# Day 21

## REJOICED OVER WITH SINGING

---

**Scripture**

Zephaniah 3:17

*"The Lord your God is with you, the Mighty Warrior who saves. He will take great delight in you… He will rejoice over you with singing."*

**Focus**

Prayer is the place where we rest in His delight and listen for His song over us.

# Day 21 Devotional Reflection

This might be one of the most beautiful, overlooked promises in Scripture: God doesn't just love you—He delights in you. He rejoices over you. He sings songs of joy and celebration about you.

Let that sink in for a second. You are not merely tolerated by God. You are treasured. You are not just accepted out of obligation. You are embraced with affection. There is a divine joy attached to your very existence. Prayer is where you begin to believe that. It is the sacred place where your identity is no longer shaped by external voices, but by eternal truth.

In a world that constantly rates, ranks, and rejects, it is easy to internalize the idea that we have to earn love or approval. But God is not looking for perfection. He is looking at you with joy. He is not keeping score. He is literally singing songs. And the more time you spend with Him in prayer, the more that melody begins to rise above the noise of rejection, insecurity, and fear.

There is a song being sung over your life right now. A song of grace, hope, and joy. A song of healing and wholeness. A song that speaks to who you are and who you are becoming. Will you tune your ear to hear it? Will you let it shape how you see yourself—not just in church, but in the mirror? Prayer is the place where that chorus becomes your confidence. It is where shame is silenced, and identity is reclaimed.

Maybe you've felt dismissed lately. Maybe you've been the woman in the room who was talked over, overlooked, or underestimated. Maybe you've carried labels for years that were never yours to begin with—too emotional, too much, not enough, too broken, too quiet. But when you enter prayer, you are reminded of who you really are. You are the one He calls *Delight*. You are the one He dances over with joy. You are the one He has always seen, always chosen, always loved.

And if you ever doubt your worth, especially in seasons when the world makes you feel unseen or unworthy, remember this: you are His beloved daughter. Cherished. Celebrated. Chosen. God doesn't just sing over the idea of you. He sings over the woman you are right now, in all your complexity and beauty. In prayer, He invites you to rest not in what you do, but in who you are to Him.

Isaiah 62:5 echoes this divine joy: "*As a bridegroom rejoices over his bride, so will your God rejoice over you.*" That is the language of love, not obligation. That is the kind of affection that transforms how we walk through the world. Prayer gives us access to that love on a daily basis.

So come as you are—worn out, unsure, longing for reassurance. Let Him sing over you. Let His delight become your rest, your reset, and your renewal.

*You do not have to feel worthy. You do not have to sound poetic.*
*You just have to come.*
*One step.*
*One breath.*
*One whispered prayer.*

**And He will meet you there.**

# Day 21 Drawing Nearer

1.  How does it change my perspective to know God delights in me—not just loves me?

    _____

    _____

    _____

2.  What lies have I believed about my worth that God's song wants to correct?

    _____

    _____

    _____

3.  When was the last time I truly rested in His presence instead of striving?

    _____

    _____

    _____

4.  What does it mean to me personally to be called His cherished daughter?

    _____

    _____

    _____

**Affirmation**

I am God's beloved daughter. He delights in me, sings over me, and quiets my heart with His love.

# Day 21 Prayer

Father,

It's hard to imagine that You sing over me.
That You rejoice in me—not because of what I've
accomplished,
but simply because I belong to You.

I've spent so much time trying to be *enough*.
But You're not waiting for me to impress You.
You're already delighting in me.

Help me believe that.
Help me silence the inner critic and hear *Your* song instead.
A song of grace. Of joy. Of love that covers every insecurity.

Let Your melody drown out the noise of my past,
the accusations of the enemy,
and the weight of my own expectations.

Today, I rest in Your delight.
I sit still and let You sing over me.
I lean into the joy that doesn't have to be earned.

You are the God who dances over His daughters.
And I am one of them.

Let that truth carry me through this day.

In Jesus' name,
Amen

# Day 22

## ONE THING I ASK

**Scripture**

Psalm 27:4

*"One thing I ask from the Lord… that I may dwell in the house of the Lord all the days of my life."*

**Focus**

Prayer expresses and cultivates a singular desire to be with God.

# Day 22 Devotional Reflection

In a world pulling us in a hundred directions, David's prayer is refreshingly singular: one thing. Just one desire. To dwell with God. To be close. To stay near. No checklist. No hustle. Just presence.

Prayer is how we dwell. It is not a visit. It is home. It is where we settle into the rhythm of grace and intimacy with the Father. David knew that everything else—safety, clarity, strength, direction—flowed from this one pursuit. He did not ask first for answers, victory, or success. He asked for nearness. Because once you have that, everything else finds its rightful place.

Maybe you have been asking God for many things lately. Provision. Healing. Breakthrough. Direction. That is okay. He hears every request. But today, what if you returned to the one thing? What if you came not with a prayer list, but with a quiet heart that simply says, "God, I just want to be with You." To abide. To dwell. To sit still and be held.

As cherished daughters of God, our deepest fulfillment is not found in the multitude of our pursuits. It is found in the singular focus of His presence. In prayer, we are invited to lay aside the distractions and demands that clamor for our attention and rest in the beauty of communion with our Heavenly Father. This dwelling is not about physical space but about the posture of our hearts. It is a continual awareness and longing for God's nearness.

Maybe you are the kind of woman who is always in motion. You are dependable, strong, constantly pouring out. You get things done. You make sure others are okay. But deep down, you crave stillness. You long for a moment when you do not have to carry it all. That longing is not weakness—it is divine invitation. An invitation to stop striving and start abiding.

Think back to the moments in your life when you felt the most at peace, the most secure, the most loved. Chances are, those were times when you were acutely aware of God's presence. Prayers cultivate this awareness. It slows us down long enough to recognize what truly matters. It reminds us that our true home is not in the external achievements or circumstances of our lives but in the steadfast, unwavering love of God.

Jesus echoed David's heart in Luke 10:42 when He said of Mary, *"only one thing is needed."* While others busied themselves with service, Mary chose to sit at Jesus' feet. She chose presence over pressure. And Jesus honored her choice. That invitation remains open to you, too.

As we make dwelling with Him our "one thing," we find that everything else: our peace, our purpose, our strength, falls into place. Because when God is at the center, everything else is grounded in the unshakable foundation of His presence.

*You do not have to feel worthy. You do not have to sound poetic.*
*You just have to come.*
*One step.*
*One breath.*
*One whispered prayer.*

**And He will meet you there.**

# Day 22 Drawing Nearer

1. What distractions are keeping me from making God my "one thing"?

   _____

   _____

   _____

2. How can I create space in my daily routine to dwell more intentionally in God's presence?

   _____

   _____

3. Reflect on a time when focusing solely on God brought clarity to a complex situation. What did I learn from that experience?

   _____

   _____

   _____

4. What does it mean for me personally to dwell in the house of the Lord all the days of my life?

   _____

   _____

   _____

**Affirmation**

I choose to make dwelling in God's presence my singular desire, finding peace and purpose as His cherished daughter.

# Day 22 Prayer

Lord,

There's so much pulling at me.
Tasks, messages, people, expectations.
And it's so easy to chase *many things* while neglecting the *one
thing* that matters most—being with You.

Like David, I echo his prayer:
"One thing I ask… that I may dwell in the house of the Lord all
the days of my life."
Not visit. Not rush through.
But dwell. Stay. Settle.

God, I don't want to just "fit You in."
I want my life to revolve around You.
Help me choose presence over pressure.
Stillness over striving.
Connection over convenience.

Give me a heart that longs to linger in Your presence.
A soul that's satisfied just by being near You.
Let my quiet time become sacred ground, not another box to
check.
Let my mind rest in the security of Your nearness.

I know that when I dwell with You, everything else falls into place.
So draw me into the one thing that truly fills me.
And let my whole life become a dwelling place for Your Spirit.

In Jesus' name,
Amen

# Day 23

## STRENGTH IN THE WAITING

**Scripture**

Isaiah 40:31

*"But those who hope in the Lord will renew their strength. They will soar on wings like eagles…"*

**Focus**

Prayer is the sacred space where hope is restored, and strength is renewed.

# Day 23 Devotional Reflection

Waiting is one of the hardest things we do as women. Whether we are waiting for healing, for clarity, for reconciliation, or for a dream to be fulfilled, the in-between can feel like a wilderness. It is dry. It is long. It is lonely. It's tempting to believe that hope is naive or that strength is something we have to muster on our own. But Isaiah 40:31 offers us a different picture: those who hope in the Lord will renew their strength. Not might. Will.

This verse is not poetic fluff. It is a spiritual guarantee. God does not ask us to manufacture strength. He invites us to receive it. And that receiving begins with prayer.

Prayer is where that renewal takes place. It is not a place of performance—it is a place of presence. In prayer, we bring our weariness, our waiting, our disappointments, and our questions. And we do not have to dress them up. We simply lay them down. Prayer is not where we fix everything. It is where we remember who holds everything.

Maybe you are in a season right now where the wait feels like it is stretching you thin. You are doing your best to remain faithful, but under the surface, you feel worn out, unseen, and maybe even forgotten. Let me tell you this: you are not weak for feeling weary. You are human. And the God who created you never intended for you to carry it all alone.

Maybe you are the woman navigating the ache of infertility. Each month feels like a fresh cycle of hope and heartbreak. You try to keep your faith strong, but your heart is heavy. In prayer, you pour out your grief and longing. And while the circumstances may not change overnight, your heart begins to change. You begin to remember that your identity is not rooted in your ability to produce something. It is grounded in the truth that you are deeply loved. Fully seen. Completely held.

Psalm 27:14 reminds us, *"Wait for the Lord; be strong and take heart and wait for the Lord."* This is not passive waiting. This is active hope. It is a bold declaration that God is still writing your story, and He will not waste a single chapter. In the waiting, He is refining your faith, stretching your strength, and deepening your dependence.

Waiting can feel like a pause, but in God's hands, it is often a place of transformation. It is where we are broken open, not for destruction, but for renewal. It is where trust is no longer theoretical, but it becomes real. Tangible. Hard-earned. Holy.

Prayer doesn't always change our situation immediately, but it does change us. It lifts our eyes from what we lack to who He is. It reminds us that strength is not found in pushing through but in leaning in. It teaches us that our ability to keep going is not dependent on how much we can endure but on how much we are willing to surrender.

If you feel tired today, if your legs are shaking and your soul is sore, pause and pray. Even a whispered breath of hope is enough. Because the promise still stands. Those who hope in the Lord will renew their strength. You will walk. You will run. And yes, even in this season, you will soar.

*You do not have to feel worthy. You do not have to sound poetic.*
*You just have to come.*
*One step.*
*One breath.*
*One whispered prayer.*

**And He will meet you there.**

# Day 23 Drawing Nearer

1. What am I waiting for in this season, and how is it affecting my heart?

   _____

   _____

   _____

2. How can I bring my honest emotions into my prayer time with God?

   _____

   _____

   _____

3. Reflect on a past season of waiting. How did God meet you there?

   _____

   _____

   _____

4. What does it mean for me to "soar on wings like eagles" in my current circumstances?

   _____

   _____

   _____

## Affirmation

Even in the waiting, I am held by God. My hope is not in outcomes but in Him, and He renews my strength daily.

# Day 23 Prayer

Father,

Waiting is hard.
It stretches me, tests me, humbles me.
It exposes my fears and reveals the places where I've placed my hope.

But You said that *those who hope in the Lord will renew their strength.*
Not those who figure it all out.
Not those who rush ahead.
But those who wait—with trust.

So here I am, Lord—still waiting.
Still hoping.
Still believing that even if I don't see the answer yet, You are working behind the scenes.

Strengthen me where I'm weary.
Steady me where I feel shaky.
Remind me that You don't waste a single second of this season.

Teach me to trust You in the tension.
To find joy in the journey.
To rest even as I wait.

Let this waiting space become a worship space.
Let it transform me, not torment me.
And when the time is right, I know You will move.
But until then—I'll stay grounded in hope and renewed by
Your strength.

In Jesus' name,
Amen

# Day 24

## PEACE THAT STAYS

**Scripture**

John 14:27

*"Peace I leave with you; my peace I give you… Do not let your hearts be troubled and do not be afraid."*

**Focus**

Prayer ushers in the supernatural peace Jesus promised.

# Day 24 Devotional Reflection

When life feels loud and uncertain, when headlines are heavy and the future looks unclear, it's easy to find our hearts troubled and our minds anxious. Between the weight of responsibilities and the noise of a constantly connected world, our souls can feel like they're carrying more than they were ever meant to bear. Yet in the middle of this internal swirl, Jesus offers us a profound gift: His peace. Not the fleeting kind the world dangles in front of us. Not temporary relief or momentary distraction. But a deep, unshakable, soul-anchoring peace.

This peace is not passive. It is not a shallow calm. It is fierce. It is rooted in the authority of Christ and held in the hands of a Savior who has already overcome the world. When Jesus spoke these words to His disciples, He was preparing them for turbulence, not ease. But He wanted them to know they would never face chaos alone. His peace would go with them.

Maybe you are a woman who feels deeply connected to the brokenness of the world. You are informed, you are engaged, and you are trying to hold it all in tension—your convictions, your compassion, your call to make a difference. But somewhere along the way, the constant intake has turned into spiritual exhaustion. You scroll before you pray. You debate before you discern. And your heart, though sincere, feels heavy and anxious.

But what if you chose a different rhythm? One where you still care deeply and stay informed, but you start with prayer instead of panic. You open your hands instead of clenching your jaw. You still vote, speak, and show up—but you do so from a place of peace, not pressure. You begin each day not with updates from the news, but with alignment in God's Word. And slowly, the atmosphere within you begins to change.

Philippians 4:6–7 reminds us of this sacred exchange: "*Do not be anxious about anything, but in every situation, by prayer and petition, with thanksgiving, present your requests to God.*" And here comes the promise: "*The peace of God, which transcends all understanding, will guard your hearts and your minds in Christ Jesus.*" That kind of peace cannot be explained—it has to be experienced. And it is available every time we pray.

Prayer doesn't remove the storms of life, but it anchors us in the middle of them. It is where we exchange our anxiety for His assurance. Our fear for His faithfulness. Our worry for His presence. And the more time we spend in that sacred space, the more our peace is no longer dependent on external conditions. It becomes rooted in the character of Christ Himself.

Jesus never promised us a life free from trouble. But He did promise that in the middle of it, we could still know peace. And not just any peace—*His* peace. The kind that keeps us grounded when the world around us is shaking. The kind that helps us show up with compassion instead of combat. The kind that settles our spirit even when nothing around us is settled.

So today, when the noise rises and the tension builds, pause. Breathe. Pray. Let His peace cover you like a warm blanket, guarding your heart and quieting your mind. You do not have to live in reaction mode. You were created to live in rest.

*You do not have to feel worthy. You do not have to sound poetic.*
*You just have to come.*
*One step.*
*One breath.*
*One whispered prayer.*

**And He will meet you there.**

# Day 24 Drawing Nearer

1. What current events or situations are causing me anxiety or fear?

   _____

   _____

   _____

2. How have I been trying to manage these concerns on my own?

   _____

   _____

   _____

3. In what ways can I invite God's peace into these areas through prayer?

   _____

   _____

   _____

4. How does trusting in God's sovereignty change my perspective on worldly events?

   _____

   _____

   _____

**Affirmation**
In the midst of turmoil, I choose to anchor my heart in God's unshakable peace, trusting that He is sovereign over all.

# Day 24 Prayer

Lord Jesus,

You said, *"Peace I leave with you, My peace I give you."*
And oh how I need that peace—not just in flashes, but in
fullness.
Not just when things are calm, but when they're completely out
of control.

The world offers a temporary calm.
But You offer an anchor.
A holy stillness that steadies me when everything around me
feels unstable.

So I receive it now—Your peace.
The kind that guards my heart.
The kind that hushes my anxiety.
The kind that fills my lungs when I can barely breathe.

Help me not just pray for peace, help me *live from it.*
Let it shape my reactions, my decisions, my posture.
Let it be the atmosphere of my home, my heart, and my
relationships.

You are the Prince of Peace.

And when You reign in me, fear has no power.

So I surrender every troubled thought to You now.

Let Your peace stay.

Let it linger.

Let it lead me.

In Jesus' name,

Amen

# Day 25

## BOLD, CLEAR, AND FEAR-FREE

**Scripture**

2 Timothy 1:7

*"For God has not given us a spirit of fear, but of power and love and a sound mind."*

**Focus**

Prayer clears the clutter of fear and activates boldness, love, and clarity.

# Day 25 Devotional Reflection

Fear can be a formidable barrier, especially when it comes to expressing our faith or standing up for what is right. The apprehension of being judged, misunderstood, or rejected often silences our voices and stifles our actions. Fear tells us to shrink back, to play it safe, to blend in and stay quiet. But 2 Timothy 1:7 reminds us that such fear does not originate from God. Instead, He endows us with power, love, and a sound mind. Our Father equips us with tools that are designed to embolden us.

This verse is more than comfort. It is a commissioning. God is not only calling us to boldness, but He is also equipping us for it. Power to speak. Love to connect. Wisdom to discern. These are not qualities we have to generate on our own. They are spiritual gifts given to us through the Holy Spirit. And prayer is how we access them.

Maybe you are a woman who has felt a holy nudge to share your faith with a friend, a coworker, or even a family member. But every time you get close, something holds you back. You start imagining the awkwardness, the judgment, the labels that might follow. You worry about being misunderstood or coming across the wrong way. So instead of stepping forward, you hold back. And afterward, you're left with that quiet regret—knowing you had something to say but let fear close your mouth.

But here's what changes everything: you take it to God in prayer. You do not pray for perfection. You pray for presence. You ask Him for the courage to obey, for the words to speak, and for the grace to love well. And slowly, your fear begins to shrink. Not because the situation becomes easier, but because your spirit becomes stronger. You start to see that moment not as a minefield of risk but as a doorway of opportunity. Prayer shifts your posture. It fills you with clarity. It reminds you that your job is to plant the seed—God will handle the soil.

Acts 4:31 says, *"After they prayed, the place where they were meeting was shaken. And they were all filled with the Holy Spirit and spoke the word of God boldly."* Notice the order. They prayed, and then they spoke. Boldness was not their default—it was the result of their time in God's presence.

Prayer doesn't eliminate the challenges we face, but it equips us to confront them with confidence. It shifts our focus from our limitations to God's limitless power. It reminds us that we are not responsible for controlling the outcome, only for being faithful in the moment. When we pray, we are reminded that our worth and identity are anchored in Christ. And that frees us from the paralyzing grip of fear.

Whether you are facing a hard conversation, a bold act of obedience, or simply the quiet call to speak truth in love—do not let fear lead. Let the Spirit lead. And let prayer be your preparation room.

*You do not have to feel worthy. You do not have to sound poetic.*
*You just have to come.*
*One step.*
*One breath.*
*One whispered prayer.*

**And He will meet you there.**

# Day 25 Drawing Nearer

1.  What fears are currently hindering me from obeying God's call?

    _____

    _____

    _____

2.  How have I experienced God's power and love in past situations where I stepped out in faith?

    _____

    _____

    _____

3.  In what areas of my life do I need to replace fear with a sound mind?

    _____

    _____

    _____

4.  How can I cultivate a prayer life that consistently reinforces my courage and clarity?

    _____

    _____

    _____

**Affirmation**

I am not governed by fear but empowered by God's spirit of power, love, and a sound mind. Through prayer, I embrace boldness and clarity in fulfilling His calling.

# Day 25 Prayer

Heavenly Father,

You have not given me a spirit of fear—
so I refuse to live like fear is my master.
You've given me power, love, and a sound mind.
So today, I take back what fear has tried to steal from me.

No more shrinking.
No more second-guessing.
No more hiding when You've called me to step out in faith.

I ask You to ignite boldness in me.
Not arrogance, but Spirit-led confidence.
Not recklessness, but holy clarity.

Give me the courage to speak truth when it's easier to stay
silent.
To move forward when the unknown feels overwhelming.
To stand firm in who You've called me to be—even when I feel
unqualified.

Replace fear with faith.
Confusion with clarity.
Insecurity with identity.

Help me show up fully—not because I have it all together,
but because I trust the One who goes before me.

Let boldness rise.
Let truth ring out.
Let love lead every word I say and every step I take.

In Jesus' name,
Amen

# Day 26

## SEARCH ME, CLEANSE ME

**Scripture**

Psalm 139:23–24

*"Search me, God, and know my heart… See if there is any offensive way in me."*

**Focus**

Prayer opens us to reflection, cleansing, and divine realignment.

# Day 26 Devotional Reflection

It is often easier to spot the speck in someone else's eye than to notice the plank in our own. We might quickly identify resistance, sin, or lack of faith in others, yet remain oblivious to our own shortcomings. Satan, the master deceiver, capitalizes on this by whispering lies that we are doing just fine—even as we slowly drift from God's truth.

Worldliness does not always announce itself with a bang. Sometimes, it creeps in subtly. A compromised decision here, a neglected prayer there, a slow dulling of conviction. Before we know it, we've gravitated away from godliness, not out of rebellion, but by way of quiet distraction. The danger lies in the gradual nature of this drift, making it harder to recognize and more difficult to confront.

Maybe you are a woman who prides herself on having strong values, who has always tried to do the right thing. But recently, in your business or relationships, small compromises have become easier to justify. You tell yourself, "This is just how the world works." But underneath that reasoning, a quiet unease begins to stir. That inner discomfort is not condemnation—it is the gentle conviction of the Holy Spirit, inviting you back to alignment.

It is in these moments that Psalm 139:23–24 becomes a lifeline. This is not a passive verse. It is a courageous, vulnerable, and radically honest prayer. A bold invitation to God: "Shine Your light in every hidden corner. I am ready to see what You see Lord."

When we pray, "Search me, God," we are not seeking a surface-level audit. We are inviting a deep, transformative examination. We are asking God to reveal not just overt sins, but also the subtle attitudes, judgments, fears, and pride that quietly steer us off course. This kind of introspection requires humility and a willingness to confront truths we may not want to admit. But it is in this holy confrontation that restoration begins.

And here is the beauty of this prayer: it does not end with exposure. It ends with direction. "Lead me in the way everlasting." God does not expose to shame. He reveals to heal. He corrects to protect. Through prayer, we experience cleansing and realignment. We shed the weights that hinder our spiritual journey and receive the grace to walk lighter, freer, and more fully awake to His presence.

As cherished daughters of God, let us embrace the courage to be searched. Let us trust that when God examines our hearts, He does so as a loving Father, not a harsh judge. In His presence, we find the grace to confront our failings and the strength to walk anew in His ways. There is no safer place to be unmasked than in the hands of the One who already knows us completely—and loves us anyway.

*You do not have to feel worthy. You do not have to sound poetic.*
*You just have to come.*
*One step.*
*One breath.*
*One whispered prayer.*

**And He will meet you there.**

# Day 26 Drawing Nearer

1. Are there areas in my life where I've become desensitized to sin or compromise?

_____

_____

_____

2. What fears or anxieties might be preventing me from inviting God's scrutiny?

_____

_____

_____

3. How have I experienced God's guidance after acknowledging and repenting of specific shortcomings?

_____

_____

_____

4. What steps can I take to remain aligned with God's path daily?

_____

_____

_____

**Affirmation**

I choose to invite God's examination, trusting that His insights lead me to growth, freedom, and deeper alignment with His will.

# Day 26 Prayer

Lord,

I don't want to play the part of holy while secretly harboring hurt, pride, or sin.
So I invite You in—into every corner of my heart.
Into the things I've ignored, justified, or hidden from myself.

Search me, God.
Know me.
Reveal anything in me that's offensive, prideful, bitter, or unbelieving.

I don't want to be blind to the ways I'm drifting from You.
Convict me—not to shame me, but to shape me.
Cleanse my thoughts. Cleanse my habits. Cleanse my motives.

I don't want surface-level change.
I want a heart that's truly transformed.
A spirit that's aligned with Yours.
A life that reflects Your holiness—not just in public, but in private.

Lead me in the way everlasting.
Guide me back when I wander.

Forgive me where I've failed.

And help me grow in grace, humility, and truth.

Thank You for loving me too much to leave me the same.

In Jesus' name,

Amen

# Day 27

## WHOLEHEARTED PURSUIT

**Scripture**

Deuteronomy 4:29

*"If you seek the Lord your God, you will find him if you seek him with all your heart and with all your soul."*

**Focus**

Prayer is a wholehearted pursuit – and God promises to be found.

# Day 27 Devotional Reflection

Modern life pulls hard on every corner of our attention. Between responsibilities at home, demands at work, the emotional energy we give to relationships, and the constant noise of our phones, it is easy to find ourselves spiritually scattered—going through the motions while feeling completely disconnected from God. We might still pray, still show up for church, still say the right things. But underneath, our hearts are tired. Drifting. Divided.

Yet even in the middle of this whirlwind, there is a divine invitation: *Seek Me.* Not half-heartedly. Not when it's convenient. Not in the leftover hours of the day. But with *all your heart and all your soul.* This is not a casual call. This is a holy challenge. A summons to deeper devotion and complete surrender.

Maybe you have reached a point in your faith where you can admit this: you have been busy with spiritual activity, but something essential has gone quiet. The fire feels dim. The joy feels faint. You love God—but if you're honest, your pursuit of

Him has slipped into autopilot. That realization is not shameful. It is sacred. Because awareness is the beginning of awakening.

What if today you drew a line in the sand and said, "No more halfway faith"? What if you began to seek God not just for what He can do, but because you want to know Him—*really* know Him? This kind of pursuit will not happen by accident. It requires intention. It means carving out space to pray, not because it's on your list, but because your soul longs for it. It means opening your Bible with expectation, worshiping even when it feels inconvenient, and choosing presence over distraction.

Wholehearted seeking doesn't mean being perfect. It means being **present**. It is waking up each day and deciding—again and again—to make God your first thought, your steady pursuit, your daily priority. God is not hiding. He is waiting. Waiting to meet you in the quiet. Waiting to stir your spirit again. Waiting to become more than a routine. Waiting to be your everything.

James 4:8 says, *"Draw near to God and he will draw near to you."* That is a promise. When we show up—even with clumsy prayers or shaky faith—He responds. He honors every attempt to know Him better. He meets hunger with holy presence. And He transforms hearts that are willing to chase after Him.

Wholehearted seeking is also active. It is more than a wishful intention—it is a daily choice. It is choosing silence over scrolling. Choosing solitude over busyness. Choosing to lean in when it would be easier to zone out. The more we chase after Him, the more we realize we were never the ones doing the chasing. He's been pursuing us all along.

**This is the essence of Deuteronomy 4:29.** It's not about a half-hearted search or a casual glance in God's direction. It's about a passionate, all-in pursuit. And the beautiful promise is that when we seek Him wholeheartedly, we *will* find Him.

**Prayer becomes the vehicle for this pursuit.** It's in the quiet moments, the honest confessions, and the earnest pleas that we draw near to God. And as we do, He meets us with open arms, ready to reveal Himself in profound and personal ways.

If your faith has felt flat, if your spirit feels dull, let this be the wake-up call. God is not calling you to check another spiritual box. He is calling you into a relationship that consumes your heart, soul, and mind. He is inviting you to lay down everything that has distracted and divided you—and come back to the *one thing* that will truly satisfy: *Him*.

*You do not have to feel worthy. You do not have to sound poetic.*
*You just have to come.*
*One step.*
*One breath.*
*One whispered prayer.*

**And He will meet you there.**

# Day 27 Drawing Nearer

1. Are there areas in my life where I've been seeking fulfillment apart from God?

   _____

   _____

   _____

2. What does it look like for me to seek God with all my heart and soul?

   _____

   _____

   _____

3. How can I make my prayer life more intentional and heartfelt?

   _____

   _____

   _____

4. In what ways has God revealed Himself to me when I've pursued Him wholeheartedly?

   _____

   _____

   _____

**Affirmation**

I choose to seek God with all my heart and soul, trusting that as I draw near to Him, He will draw near to me.

# Day 27 Prayer

Heavenly Father,

You promised that if I seek You with all my heart, I will find
You.
So today, I'm not holding back.
No more halfway devotion. No more partial obedience.
You deserve my *whole* heart.

I want to pursue You with the same passion I give to everything
else.
I want to long for You more than I long for answers.
To desire You more than I desire comfort, success, or applause.

Help me be intentional. Consistent. Focused.
When the distractions come—and they always do—remind me
what matters most.

Let my life be marked by pursuit.
Not perfection, but passion.
Not busyness, but nearness.

And when I seek You in prayer, in stillness, in worship,
let me find You waiting—ready to reveal more of Yourself.

You are the treasure I'm after.

And I will keep running toward You, one step at a time, one prayer at a time.

You are worth it all.

In Jesus' name,
Amen

# Day 28

## COME WEARY, LEAVE RENEWED

**Scripture**

Matthew 11:28–29

*"Come to me, all you who are weary and burdened, and I will give you rest."*

**Focus**

Prayer is where we come weary and leave renewed.

# Day 28 Devotional Reflection

Motherhood is a beautiful, sacred calling. It is also relentless. From sleepless nights with a newborn to the nonstop motion of toddlerhood, to school drop-offs, work meetings, dinner prep, and the never-ending mental checklist of "What's next?"—being a mother often means pouring out every ounce of yourself for someone else. And as noble and holy as that may be, it can leave you utterly depleted.

In the blur of busyness and the heartache of 'not-enoughness,' Jesus extends a gentle but urgent invitation: *Come to me, and I will give you rest.* Not just a nap. Not just help with the to-do list. But deep, soul-renewing rest. A stillness that settles your spirit. A peace that does not depend on the kids behaving or the kitchen being clean. A strength that lifts you up, even when no one else notices you're falling apart.

But here's the truth many mothers hesitate to admit we often resist that invitation. We love our children so much that we put everything else, including ourselves and our relationship with God on hold. We tell ourselves, *"I'll pray later. I'll rest later. I'll breathe later."* But later never comes, and the cycle of burnout continues. We run on fumes and call it faithfulness. We ignore our soul and call it sacrifice.

The problem is not our love for our children. The problem is the belief that we must do it all alone.

Maybe you're a mother who hasn't had a quiet moment in days. Your Bible sits unopened, your prayers are fragmented thoughts between carpool and chaos, and your heart feels far from steady. But this is exactly where Jesus wants to meet you—not when it's calm, but right in the crazy. You don't need a silent room and candle-lit worship to connect with God. You just need a moment. A breath. A whispered, *"Help me, Lord."*

That moment matters. That breath is sacred.

Prayer in motherhood may not look like an hour of solitude. It may look like praying while you fold laundry or speaking scriptures over your child's fevered forehead. It may look like crying in the shower or repeating a single verse while packing lunches. And yes, God meets you *there*. Right there.

Isaiah 40:11 says, *"He gently leads those that have young."* That means He is not demanding or impatient with mothers. He is gentle. He understands. He sees every sacrifice, every sleepless night, every silent tear. And He's not asking you to carry the weight of motherhood alone—He's asking you to come to Him so He can carry *you*.

You are not just a mother. You are a daughter of the Most High God. And your soul matters, too. Your spirit deserves nourishment. You cannot pour living water into your children if your own well has run dry. That is not selfish. That is stewardship.

So Mama, today is your invitation. Come to Jesus. Lay it down— the guilt, the pressure, the perfectionism. Let Him be the rhythm behind your routines and the peace beneath your pressure. Let Him remind you that your worth is not in how much you do, but in how deeply you are loved.

*You do not have to feel worthy. You do not have to sound poetic.*
*You just have to come.*
*One step.*
*One breath.*
*One whispered prayer.*

**And He will meet you there.**

# Day 28 Drawing Nearer

1. What burdens am I carrying today that I need to lay at Jesus' feet?

   _____

   _____

   _____

2. How can I create moments of rest and connection with God amidst my daily routine?

   _____

   _____

   _____

3. In what ways have I experienced God's renewal in past seasons of weariness?

   _____

   _____

   _____

4. What scriptures can I meditate on to remind me of God's promise of rest?

   _____

   _____

   _____

**Affirmation**

Even in my exhaustion, I am held by God's grace. He renews my strength and fills me with His peace.

# Day 28 Prayer

Lord Jesus,

You said, "Come to Me, all who are weary and burdened, and I will give you rest."
So here I am, Lord.
Tired. Carrying more than I was meant to.
Doing my best to keep it together but feeling like I'm unraveling.

I need the kind of rest only You can give.
Not just a nap. Not a distraction. But soul-deep *renewal*.

Lift the weight I've been dragging around.
Remind me that it's okay to pause.
To be poured into.
To simply *be* with You.

You don't require perfection before You pour out peace.
You invite me as I am—exhausted and unfinished—and promise rest for my soul.

So, I lay it all down:
The pressure.
The guilt.
The silent expectations I've placed on myself.

Refresh me, God.
Renew my energy.
Restore my joy.
Revive my spirit.

Let me leave this moment lighter than I came.
Not because my problems are gone,
but because I've placed them in Your hands.

In Jesus' name,
Amen

# Day 29

## IN HIS PRESENCE IS FULLNESS

**Scripture**

Psalm 16:11

*"You make known to me the path of life; in your presence there is fullness of joy…"*

**Focus**

Prayer brings us into the presence where joy overflows.

# Day 29 Devotional Reflection

Depression can feel like a relentless fog, dimming the light of joy and making each day a struggle. It doesn't always look like tears. Sometimes it looks like numbness. Sometimes it sounds like silence. For many women, this battle is fought quietly—behind the carpool line, behind flawless Instagram posts, behind polite smiles and checked-off to-do lists. But beneath it all is a silent ache. A fatigue of the soul.

And yet, even in the depths of despair, God's promise stands firm: *in His presence, there is fullness of joy.*

That joy is not performative. It's not loud or showy. It is not the fake-it-til-you-make-it cheerfulness the world pushes. This joy is sacred. Rooted. Holy. It is not the absence of sorrow—it is the presence of God right in the middle of the sorrow.

Maybe you are the woman who has been pressing on in faith while secretly walking through darkness. You've prayed, but nothing feels different. You still feel heavy. Your joy feels far away. Some days, getting out of bed is your victory. And on those days, you wonder if God sees you. If He is near. If joy is even possible again.

But hear this: yes, He sees you. Yes, He is near. And yes, joy is still possible.

You do not have to bring eloquent prayers. You do not have to pretend. Your tears, your silence, your sighs—they all count as prayer. Romans 8:26 says that when we do not know what to pray, the Spirit Himself intercedes for us with groans too deep for words. That means even when you cannot speak, heaven still hears.

Picture this: you sit quietly, your heart aching, words stuck in your throat. But you still come to God. That *choice* to enter His presence, even without the feelings and even without the answers, is an act of holy defiance against despair. And in those moments, something begins to shift. Not always quickly. Not always visibly. But it starts. A flicker of hope. A breath of peace. A whisper of reassurance: *You're not alone.*

This is how joy begins to take root—not as a flash of happiness, but as a slow, steady unfolding of light within the darkness. Prayers do not always change the situation immediately. But it transforms you. It gives you the strength to keep standing, even when everything around you says to fall.

Psalm 30:5 says, "*Weeping may stay for the night, but rejoicing comes in the morning.*" But sometimes that "morning" takes longer than we want. Still, it comes. Slowly. Softly. Surely. And when you stay in God's presence, even through the night, joy becomes more than a feeling. It becomes your lifeline.

So dear sister, let go of the pressure to feel okay. God is not asking you to *feel* joy before you come. He is asking you to *come*, so He can *fill* you with it. One moment at a time. One breath at a time.

Joy isn't the absence of sorrow. It is the presence of God amid your pain. It is the knowing that you are seen, loved, and held. Even when your soul feels fragile, His joy is your strength.

*You do not have to feel worthy. You do not have to sound poetic.*
*You just have to come.*
*One step.*
*One breath.*
*One whispered prayer.*

**And He will meet you there.**

# Day 29 Drawing Nearer

1. What aspects of my life feel joyless right now?

   _____

   _____


2. How have I experienced God's presence in past struggles?

   _____

   _____


3. What scriptures can I meditate on to remind me of God's promises?

   _____

   _____


4. In what ways can I cultivate moments of joy, even in small things?

   _____

   _____

   _____


**Affirmation**

Even in my darkest moments, God's presence offers me joy and hope. I choose to seek Him, trusting that His joy will sustain me.

# Day 29 Prayer

Lord,

In the midst of my depression, I seek Your presence.
For You are the source of true joy.
Not the temporary kind that fades when the moment passes,
but a joy that lives deep in my bones—even when life is hard.
Even when I feel heavy. Even when nothing around me
changes.

Your Word says, *"In Your presence there is fullness of joy."*
And oh, how I need that kind of joy—not circumstantial, but
spiritual.
Joy that rises from knowing I'm not alone.
Joy that anchors me when I'm anxious.
Joy that's rooted in You, not my reality.

Some days joy feels far away—when grief lingers, when
depression presses in,
when I wonder if things will ever feel light again.
But I believe Your joy meets me even there.
Not because I fake a smile, but because I find You in the
shadows.

So I press into Your presence.
I quiet the chaos, and I come close.

I bring my sadness. My silence. My need.
And I trust You to fill the empty places with something holy.

Thank You for joy that overflows even in sorrow.
For laughter that returns. For peace that stays.
Let Your joy be my strength today and every day.

In You—I am whole. I am held.
And I am filled.


In Jesus' name,
Amen

# Day 30

## HEARTS BURNING WITHIN

**Scripture**

Luke 24:32

*"Were not our hearts burning within us while he talked with us on the road and opened the Scriptures to us?"*

**Focus**

That holy heartburning still happens in prayer when He speaks and we listen.

# Day 30 Devotional Reflection

There's something holy about hoping for love—and praying for it boldly.

In a culture that can make singleness feel like a waiting room, it's easy to wonder if your desire for a godly relationship is too much, too late, or somehow in vain. But here's the truth, sis: God isn't intimidated by your longing. He's not rolling His eyes at your prayers. He's listening. He's working. And He's not just preparing someone—He's preparing you both.

The disciples on the road to Emmaus were confused, hurting, and walking forward with no clear direction. But that's where Jesus showed up. He didn't fix everything in an instant. He walked with them. He talked with them. And as He spoke, their hearts burned within them. That kind of moment? It's what happens when presence meets expectation.

You can walk your own Emmaus road—asking questions, feeling unseen, wondering when love will come—and still believe Jesus is right beside you. You can bring Him your ache for connection and your vision for partnership. You can pray, not just in general terms, but with specific faith: for a man after God's heart. For shared purpose. For deep spiritual chemistry. For emotional maturity and Christlike love. These aren't silly requests. They are sacred petitions—and God honors them.

Maybe you're that woman. Strong in your faith, but honest about the ache. Surrounded by people yet still craving your person. You've gone to the weddings. You've played bridesmaid. You've smiled through the advice. But behind closed doors, you've wondered if God skipped you.

He didn't.

You are not forgotten. You are not overlooked. And your desire to be loved by someone who loves God is not small—it's strategic. It's prophetic. It's part of your story.

This season isn't punishment—it's preparation. So instead of praying to stop wanting it, pray to grow into it. Ask God to refine your heart, deepen your trust, and protect the kind of love that's worth waiting for. And while you wait, don't shrink. Don't settle. Don't apologize for having high standards and a holy desire.

Let your prayers evolve. Let them get specific. Let them ask for character, not just chemistry. And let them start with this: "God, make me the kind of woman who is ready for the kind of man I'm praying for."

When that becomes your prayer, something shifts. Your focus moves from "when will he come?" to "who am I becoming?" And just like those disciples, your heart begins to burn—not with desperation, but with expectancy.

So no, this season doesn't define you. But it does shape you. And when the time comes, you won't just be a woman who waited. You'll be a woman who prayed with fire, grew with grace, and walked with Jesus until the love He ordained found its way to your door.

Let your hope be loud. Let your prayers be specific.

And let your heart burn—not just for love, but for the One who is Love.

*You do not have to feel worthy. You do not have to sound poetic. You just have to come.*
*One step.*
*One breath.*
*One whispered prayer.*

**And He will meet you there.**

# Day 30 Drawing Nearer

1.  What specific qualities am I praying for in a future partner—and how do they reflect God's heart?

    _____

    _____

    _____

2.  In what ways is God using this season of singleness to grow, refine, or prepare me?

    _____

    _____

    _____

3.  How can I shift from passive waiting to active preparation—spiritually, emotionally, and relationally?

    _____

    _____

    _____

4.  Am I willing to trust God with both the timing and the outcome of my desire for love?

    _____

    _____

    _____

**Affirmation**

I am already loved, being prepared in grace, held in wholeness, and waiting with wonder for the love God is shaping—for me and within me.

# Day 30 Prayer

God of holy timing, of sacred love stories, of details I'll never see,

Here I am. Single. Waiting. Believing. Some days strong, some days weary, some days unsure if the kind of love I'm praying for even exists. But today, I choose to believe again.

I bring You my ache, not as a complaint, but as an offering. The lonely nights, the heavy questions, the well-meaning advice, the invisible pressure to "be okay." You see it all. You hold it all. And still, You invite me to draw near—not because I'm whole, but because I'm Yours.

God, I won't settle for vague hope. I'm praying bold and specific. Prepare the heart of the man I'm praying for—even now. Shape his character. Strengthen his faith. Teach him to lead in love and humility. Surround him with wise counsel and protect him from the distractions of this world. Let his desire for You be louder than any desire for applause.

And while You're preparing him, prepare me too. Not just to be loved, but to love well. To forgive quickly. To speak life. To walk in wholeness. To carry grace in my mouth and purpose in my stride. Let me become a safe place, a prayer warrior, a joyful partner—not just a woman waiting for a ring, but a woman being refined for a covenant.

Heal the places in me that still feel unseen or unworthy. Silence the voice that says I'm too late or not enough. Remind me that I am not a backup plan—I am chosen, called, and cherished by the Most High. And You don't make mistakes.

Let this season be one of sacred preparation. Let it stretch my faith, enlarge my joy, and deepen my intimacy with You. Not because singleness is my identity, but because this season has purpose.

I refuse to shrink. I refuse to settle. I refuse to doubt that the God who authored love itself would somehow forget about mine. So, I will pray with passion. I will grow with grace. I will walk with confidence. And I will wait—not in fear, but in fire.

In Jesus' name, I pray for more than love—I pray for destiny.

Amen.

# Conclusion

As we close this 30-day journey, remember—prayer is not just a chapter you complete. It's a rhythm you carry. A lifeline you hold. A daily invitation to dwell in the presence of the One who knows you best and loves you most.

Every season of life holds its own beauty, its own battles, and its own beckoning to draw near. Wherever you are—on the mountaintop, in the waiting, or in the quiet middle—God is there, ready to meet you.

Don't rush past this moment. Let your soul settle. Let your spirit breathe. And let your heart stay ablaze with His love, anchored in His truth, and forever reaching for more of Him.

Heavenly Father Up Above,

Thank You!

For the moments You whispered in stillness,
and the times You thundered through my fear.
For every verse that pierced, every prayer that soothed,
every moment that reminded me—I am Yours.

These past 30 days were not just a devotional.
They were a journey. A return. A rebuilding. A drawing near.

Thank You for meeting me in my ordinary days and
transforming them into sacred spaces.
For showing me that intimacy with You isn't for the perfect—
it's for the willing.
For proving again that when I move toward You, You're
already running toward me.

Seal every truth in my heart.
Strengthen every seed You've planted.
And stir in me a hunger for even more.

Let this be my new rhythm—not an ending, but a beginning.
A daily invitation to draw near and dwell.

Keep me tethered to Your Word.
Anchored in Your peace.

Bold in prayer.
Soft in heart.

And above all else—keep me close.

This journey has changed me.

In Jesus Holy Name,
Amen.

# Appendix I

## God's Promises – A Scripture Reference Guide

When life moves fast and your heart feels heavy, come back to this sacred space. These scriptures are here to steady your soul, speak truth into the fog, and remind you that God is still with you—still providing, still guiding, still faithful.

Whether you are needing peace, strength, direction, or simply a reason to hope, His Word is your anchor. Let these promises lead you back into prayer whenever you need to remember: *He is enough.*

### Provision

**When you're not sure how the needs will be met—whether it's bills, energy, time, or peace of mind—remember: God is a generous provider, not a reluctant one. His supply never runs dry.**

*"And my God will meet all your needs according to the riches of his glory in Christ Jesus."*
—Philippians 4:19 (NIV)

## Peace

**When the world feels loud, your thoughts race, or anxiety grips your chest—pause. Breathe. You're not alone. God offers peace that the world can't manufacture, and chaos can't cancel.**

*"You will keep in perfect peace all who trust in you, all whose thoughts are fixed on you!"*
—Isaiah 26:3 (NLT)

## Strength

**When you feel weary, stretched thin, or flat-out done, take heart: your weakness is not the end—it's the beginning of God's power working in you.**

*"Don't panic. I'm with you. There's no need to fear for I'm your God. I'll give you strength. I'll help you. I'll hold you steady, keep a firm grip on you."*
—Isaiah 41:10 (MSG)

## Guidance

**When you're standing at a crossroads, unsure of what to do or where to go, lean into the God who sees the full picture. He's not just willing to guide you—He delights in it.**

*"Trust in the Lord with all your heart and lean not on your own understanding;*
*In all your ways acknowledge Him, and He shall direct your paths."*
—Proverbs 3:5–6 (NKJV)

### Faithfulness

**When doubt creeps in or you feel like you've messed up beyond repair, rest in this truth: God's faithfulness isn't based on your performance—it's rooted in His character.**

*"If we are faithless, He remains faithful, for He cannot deny Himself."*
—2 Timothy 2:13 (NASB)

### Hope

**When discouragement clouds your vision or the wait feels too long, hope reminds you that God is still working—often in the unseen. His promises are never empty.**

*"Let us hold unswervingly to the hope we profess, for he who promised is faithful."*
—Hebrews 10:23 (NIV)

## Healing

**When your body aches, your heart breaks, or your spirit feels wounded, cling to the One who heals deeply, tenderly, and completely—in His time and in His way.**

*"But I will restore you to health and heal your wounds," declares the Lord.*
—Jeremiah 30:17 (NIV)


## Forgiveness

**When guilt whispers lies, and shame tries to linger, remember grace has the final word. God's forgiveness is not partial—its complete, restoring what sin tried to steal.**

*"If we confess our sins, He is faithful and just to forgive us our sins and to cleanse us from all unrighteousness."*
—1 John 1:9 (NKJV)


## Identity

**When you're tempted to shrink back or question your worth, let God remind you: you are chosen, beloved, and created with divine intention.**

*"You are my child, chosen and marked by my love, the pride of my life."*
—Matthew 3:17 (MSG)

Joy

**When life feels heavy or happiness seems out of reach, remember joy isn't dependent on your circumstances, it's rooted in His presence.**

*"You make known to me the path of life; in your presence there is fullness of joy; at your right hand are pleasures forevermore."*
—Psalm 16:11 (ESV)

# Appendix II

## Powerful Prayers from the Bible

Prayer has always been the heart-cry of God's people. From barren wombs to repentant kings, angel visits to prison cells, Scripture is filled with honest, raw, and faith-filled prayers. These passages remind us that God hears us—whether we whisper in sorrow or shout in joy. Use these powerful prayers to guide your own conversations with Him, echoing the voices of those who've walked the path before you.

### Hannah's Prayer for a Child

1 Samuel 1:10–11 (NLT)

*"Hannah was in deep anguish, crying bitterly as she prayed to the Lord. And she made this vow: 'O Lord of Heaven's Armies, if you will look upon my sorrow and answer my prayer and give me a son, then I will give him back to you.'"*

This prayer teaches us to pour out our longings honestly before God, trusting that He sees the ache and honors surrendered faith.

### David's Prayer of Repentance

Psalm 51 (ESV)

*"Create in me a clean heart, O God, and renew a right spirit within me... The sacrifices of God are a broken spirit; a broken and contrite heart, O God, you will not despise."*

David models what it looks like to return to God in the aftermath of failure—raw, humbled, yet anchored in the belief that God's mercy is greater than our mistakes.

### Mary's Song of Surrender

Luke 1:46–55 (NIV)

*"My soul glorifies the Lord and my spirit rejoices in God my Savior... for the Mighty One has done great things for me—holy is his name."*

Mary's prayer is a song of awe and surrender, reminding us to praise God not only for what He's done, but for who He is—even when the road ahead is unknown.

### Jesus' High Priestly Prayer

John 17 (NKJV)

*"I do not pray for these alone, but also for those who will believe in Me through their word... that they all may be one, as You, Father, are in Me, and I in You."*

Jesus' final recorded prayer before the cross reveals His deepest desire—for unity, for protection, for intimacy between God and His people. This prayer covers you, even now.

**Paul's Prayer for the Ephesians**

Ephesians 3:14–21 (MSG)

*"I ask him to strengthen you by his Spirit—not a brute strength but a glorious inner strength—that Christ will live in you as you open the door and invite him in."*

Paul's prayer is a powerful blessing over the believer's inner life. It invites us into deeper roots, wider love, and the boundless fullness of God.

# Appendix III

## Scriptures from the Journey

Each day of this devotional began with a whisper from God's Word—a verse to center your heart and anchor your prayers. Here, you'll find those 30 scriptures gathered in one place. Revisit them as a personal reading plan, write them in your journal, or let one speak into your spirit when you need a reminder of His nearness.

---

**Day 1 – James 4:8 (NIV)**
*"Come near to God and he will come near to you."*

**Day 2 – Psalm 46:10 (NLT)**
*"Be still, and know that I am God! I will be honored by every nation. I will be honored throughout the world."*

**Day 3 – John 10:27 (MSG)**
*"My sheep recognize my voice. I know them, and they follow me."*

**Day 4 – Micah 6:8 (ESV)**
*"He has told you, O man, what is good; and what does the Lord*

*require of you but to do justice, and to love kindness, and to walk humbly with your God?"*

### Day 5 – Romans 5:5 (NIV)
*"God's love has been poured out into our hearts through the Holy Spirit, who has been given to us."*

### Day 6 – Psalm 37:4 (NKJV)
*"Delight yourself also in the Lord, and He shall give you the desires of your heart."*

### Day 7 – Isaiah 26:3 (NLT)
*"You will keep in perfect peace all who trust in you, all whose thoughts are fixed on you!"*

### Day 8 – Hebrews 11:6 (NIV)
*"And without faith it is impossible to please God... he rewards those who earnestly seek him."*

### Day 9 – Psalm 51:17 (ESV)
*"The sacrifices of God are a broken spirit; a broken and contrite heart, O God, you will not despise."*

### Day 10 – John 15:4 (NKJV)
*"Abide in Me, and I in you. As the branch cannot bear fruit of itself, unless it abides in the vine, neither can you, unless you abide in Me."*

### Day 11 - Romans 8:38–39 (NIV)

*"Nothing… will be able to separate us from the love of God that is in Christ Jesus our Lord."*

### Day 12 - Matthew 5:8 (NLT)

*"God blesses those whose hearts are pure, for they will see God."*

### Day 13 - Psalm 63:1 (MSG)

*"God—you're my God! I can't get enough of you! I've worked up such hunger and thirst for God, traveling across dry and weary deserts."*

### Day 14 - 2 Corinthians 3:18 (NIV)

*"We… are being transformed into his image with ever-increasing glory, which comes from the Lord, who is the Spirit."*

### Day 15 - Philippians 3:10 (NLT)

*"I want to know Christ and experience the mighty power that raised him from the dead. I want to suffer with him, sharing in his death."*

### Day 16 - Ezekiel 36:26 (NKJV)

*"I will give you a new heart and put a new spirit within you…"*

### Day 17 - Proverbs 3:5–6 (MSG)

*"Trust God from the bottom of your heart; don't try to figure out everything on your own. Listen for God's voice in everything you do…"*

**Day 18 – Colossians 3:2 (NIV)**

*"Set your minds on things above, not on earthly things."*

**Day 19 – Psalm 42:1–2 (NLT)**

*"As the deer longs for streams of water, so I long for you, O God. I thirst for God, the living God."*

**Day 20 – Galatians 2:20 (ESV)**

*"I have been crucified with Christ. It is no longer I who live, but Christ who lives in me…"*

**Day 21 – Zephaniah 3:17 (NIV)**

*"The Lord your God is with you… He will take great delight in you; in his love he will no longer rebuke you, but will rejoice over you with singing."*

**Day 22 – Psalm 27:4 (NLT)**

*"The one thing I ask of the Lord—the thing I seek most—is to live in the house of the Lord all the days of my life…"*

**Day 23 – Isaiah 40:31 (NKJV)**

*"But those who wait on the Lord shall renew their strength; they shall mount up with wings like eagles…"*

**Day 24 – John 14:27 (ESV)**

*"Peace I leave with you; my peace I give to you. Not as the world gives do I give to you. Let not your hearts be troubled, neither let them be afraid."*

### Day 25 – 2 Timothy 1:7 (NLT)

*"For God has not given us a spirit of fear and timidity, but of power, love, and self-discipline."*

### Day 26 – Psalm 139:23–24 (NIV)

*"Search me, God, and know my heart… See if there is any offensive way in me, and lead me in the way everlasting."*

### Day 27 – Deuteronomy 4:29 (NKJV)

*"But from there you will seek the Lord your God, and you will find Him if you seek Him with all your heart and with all your soul."*

### Day 28 – Matthew 11:28–29 (MSG)

*"Come to me. Get away with me and you'll recover your life… I won't lay anything heavy or ill-fitting on you. Keep company with me and you'll learn to live freely and lightly."*

### Day 29 – Psalm 16:11 (ESV)

*"You make known to me the path of life; in your presence there is fullness of joy…"*

### Day 30 – Luke 24:32 (NLT)

*"Didn't our hearts burn within us as he talked with us on the road and explained the Scriptures to us?"*

# Want to Go Deeper in Prayer?

## What's Next on Your Journey

Sister, if *Draw Near* met you in a dry place and refreshed you—or simply gave you language for the closeness you've been craving—know this: God delights in your pursuit of Him, and the journey doesn't end here.

---

## Step 1: Join the 30-Day Prayer Challenge

Grow with women from around the world in a safe, faith-filled space. Inside you'll find:

Daily scriptures and prompts

Encouragement from sisters walking the same path

A community to cheer you on

or visit: AngelaRosko.com/community

---

## Step 2: Download Your Free Gift

The *Faith-Filled Prayer Journal* is a gentle 30-day experience to help you slow down and reconnect with God in fresh, intimate ways.

or visit: AngelaRosko.com

---

## Step 3: Be the First to Know About My Next Book

### Pathways to Salvation: Walking in God's Truth, Not Religious Tradition

A bold, grace-filled guide into deeper truths of faith and walking with God in real life.

or visit: AngelaRosko.com

## Step 4: Join the Movement

Prayer doesn't stop here. I'm building spaces for women to gather and grow:

**Prayer Brunches** – soulful gatherings to rest + connect

**Women's Retreats** – weekend refreshers for faith and fellowship

**Speaking & Coaching** – let's grow together!

or visit: AngelaRosko.com/events

---

## Final Step: Spread the Word

If this book blessed you, would you…

Share it with a friend

Leave a review online

Tag me on social media

Your words help others draw near, too.

---

With love,

**Angela Rosko**

[AngelaRosko.com] | [@AngelaRosko]